I0080268

TITUS

ADORN THE WORD

© 2018 Mindi Jo Furby. All rights reserved.

No part of this book may be reproduced, stored in a retrieval system, or transmitted by any means without the written permission of the author.

First published June 2018
ISBN: 978-1-943413-09-6

Visit us on the web!
www.mindijofurby.com

Published by: KingsWynd Books

KingsWynd exists to fight biblical illiteracy in our families, church, communities, and world. Our goal is to help others love God and become more like Jesus through His Word. We accomplish this through publishing books, articles, curricula, and Bible studies used by individuals and churches throughout the world.

For more information about KingsWynd Books, visit www.kingswynd.com.

Printed in the United States of America

Scripture, unless otherwise noted, taken from the NEW AMERICAN STANDARD BIBLE®, Copyright© 1960, 1962, 1963, 1968, 1971, 1972, 1973, 1975, 1977, 1995 by The Lockman Foundation. Used by permission.

Author: Mindi Jo Furby
Edited by: Christina Miller
Cover: Emily Rogers
Formatting: Polgarus Studio

Contents

MAKE Bible Studies

The goal of every Christian is to glorify God and become more like Jesus. The process of realizing this goal is discipleship. Christ chose twelve disciples during His years of ministry on earth and commissioned them to continue the process of making disciples—of helping people become more like Him.

Since I am a disciple of Christ, my prayer is to do the same.

Some try to squeeze the process of discipleship into a concise list with check-off boxes: "read your Bible," "attend church regularly," etc. While we encourage such spiritual disciplines, by themselves they don't make disciples. We may gain knowledge, but the end product will mirror the Pharisees more than Jesus.

If we intend to become more like Jesus and help others do the same, we must do as He did. Jesus' method for discipleship was quite simple. He used relationships, fueled by God's Word, to produce disciples.

Jesus didn't instruct His disciples to check off behavioral boxes as they went about their lives. He didn't assign homework involving endless questions and intense reading before they could come back and talk to Him. He *lived* with them—pouring into their lives and using their relationships (with Him and each other) as the conduit for spiritual growth and maturity.

If that's how He produced disciples, that's how we should too.

MAKE Bible Studies exist to make disciples by igniting relationships fueled by God's Word. These studies are intensely practical and life applicable. They're intentionally designed with relationships in mind—first your relationship with God, then your relationships with others in a group setting.

MAKE studies work because they're simple and fiercely poignant. They're designed to be the launching point for discussion, action, and transformation—merging God's truth with life in practical, engaging ways. Be as involved as you want. You have the option of engaging in the personal Bible study and commentary before your group meets or simply showing up for discussion on group nights. (Homework is not necessary, though it is helpful.)

The following resources are available for your convenience: an Introduction to Titus, personal Bible study questions, passage commentaries, and group study guides for each week. A special note to group leaders: read through the commentary and study guides prior to your group meeting. Pray over the material, make notes, and think of ways to instigate further discussion. Also, before beginning every week, discuss ways your group members incorporated the prior week's challenges into their lives and faith.

Enjoy the journey of becoming more like Jesus through this study of Titus. Keep your eyes open and your heart hungry for His transforming power in your life and the lives of your group members!

Introduction to Titus

Titus. A short book in the New Testament. A book exalted by women's ministries for the popular verses in chapter two. A great book for providing guidelines for church leadership, especially the establishment of elders. A prized book to our Type A friends who like lists of moral rules. A dreaded book, perhaps, for our Type B friends who don't appreciate such structure.

Regardless, it's rich, to the point, and an easy read. Three chapters and less than ten minutes are all you need to finish this little gem. A fair warning, though: its ease leads many to shallow comprehension. It's easy to skim the surface for a fast read and just as easy to remain on the surface—missing the depths of truth God extends to us. Fortunately, it doesn't have to be that way. As with every other book in the Bible, God meticulously inspired the words of Titus, not for a quick read, but for a transformed life.

My aim and prayer for this book is exactly that—a transformation of your life (and mine) to the image of Jesus Christ as executed by the Holy Spirit and ordained by God long ago. God knew you would read this book at this specific time in your life, and if you'll open your heart and mind, I'm convinced He'll reveal His truth to you in ways you never dreamed possible. That's exactly what He's done for me. Let's refuse the superficial and embrace the profound as we dig into a book that can revolutionize our faith.

WEEK ONE
TITUS 1:1-4

PERSONAL BIBLE STUDY QUESTIONS

1. Who is the human author of this book? (1:1)

    a) What do you know about him?

2. Why is it significant that God cannot lie? (1:2)

    a) How does this fact make you feel?

    b) How can/does this fact impact your faith?

3. Who is the letter written to? (1:4)

    a) What is his relationship to the author?

    b) What are some benefits to having this kind of relationship in one's life?

        i.   Are you (or have you been) in a relationship like this, either from the author's or recipient's perspective? With whom?

COMMENTARY

> "Paul, a bond-servant of God and an apostle of Jesus Christ, for the faith of those chosen of God and the knowledge of the truth which is according to godliness, in the hope of eternal life, which God, who cannot lie, promised long ages ago, but at the proper time manifested, even His word, in the proclamation with which I was entrusted according to the commandment of God our Savior, to Titus, my true child in a common faith: Grace and peace from God the Father and Christ Jesus our Savior."
>
> Titus 1:1-4

In a world that's increasingly difficult to impress, book introductions have a difficult task. If we aren't immediately awestruck, we tend to enter "skim mode." We breeze through a text to glean what we can, then toss it aside. That's honestly not hard to do with the introduction to Titus. Huge run-on sentences are tough to keep track of (thanks, Paul). While Titus' opening lines include several impressive theological nuggets, digging them out and making them shine seems like a lot of work.

But, like much else in life, if we are willing to get our hands dirty, the reward will make our hard work a distant memory.

Let's begin!

PAUL

First words are always revealing. From the first part of our first sentence, we learn that the apostle Paul is the author of the book of Titus. Some academics have risen within the last couple of centuries to claim Paul didn't write this book (based on a lot of complicated conjecture and theory). But the majority of scholars and evangelicals today agree that Paul is, in fact, the genuine author of Titus.[1]

Fortunately, we know quite a bit about the apostle Paul. In the book of Acts, we're introduced to him as a man named Saul. Despite being a very "religious" man, Saul greatly opposed Christianity. So fierce was his opposition, he participated as a willing bystander to Stephen's murder—the first martyrdom of our faith.[2] His hatred for Christians (known then as people belonging to "the Way"[3]) only grew from there. "Ravaging the church, entering house after house, and dragging off men and women, he would put them in prison."[4] Needless to say, this man despised the church and abhorred its Lord (which is ironic, since he thought himself an upright Jew who served God faithfully[5]).

God had other plans for him, though. On his way to arrest more Christians in Damascus, Saul had a little chat with God. The event left him temporarily blind and permanently changed.[6] He stayed relatively quiet in his faith for fourteen years—resetting, being discipled, and proving he wasn't a spy trying to work his way into the inner circles of early church leadership.[7] He was truly changed. When Saul became Paul, an agent of murder became an agent of new life, and God used him awaken the world to the gospel of Jesus Christ.

Several volumes could be (and have been) written about Paul, but for our discussion, it's important to know that he pioneered world missions and established numerous churches throughout the ancient near east. His spiritual conquests brought thousands to saving faith in Jesus Christ. Many of them were documented in the books of the New Testament, of which he penned thirteen.

Knowing Paul authored Titus automatically gives the book weight. We value things written, made, worn, or even touched by people we admire. A baseball signed by Babe Ruth? Worth thousands upon thousands of dollars. One of Marilyn Monroe's dresses apparently sold for more than 4 million dollars not many years ago.[8] Those two examples are just things—a ball and a dress. They would be worthless (and probably thrown away long ago) if they'd been used by normal people. But because they came in contact with celebrities, their value increased exponentially.

Those celebrities made big splashes in our culture but brought little (if any) eternal value to our world. Paul, on the other hand, helped establish the church. He acted as a propellant to the gospel, taking it from one small location to the entire known world. Thousands, perhaps millions, of people are basking in God's presence in heaven at this very minute because of Paul's influence. All the credit, of course, goes to God for using him. But Paul was an obedient servant who identified with Christ, and we are blessed to have his writings in the canon of Scripture.

A BOND-SERVANT OF GOD AND AN APOSTLE OF JESUS CHRIST

Identity is both powerful and elusive. Powerful because our sense of identity impacts every aspect of our lives. Elusive because many people struggle to discover their identities, spending countless time, money, and energy trying to figure out who they are and what their purpose is.

The apostle Paul knew who he was. He found and secured his identity in God through Jesus Christ and spent his life helping others do the same. The phrase **bond-servant of God** here begins with the Greek word *doulos* or "servant," and is used well over a hundred times in the New Testament. But only here is it used by Paul as a self-descriptor.[9]

The concept of servanthood or slavery instinctively leaves a bad taste in our mouths because of America's horrendous, evil history of enslaving other human beings solely for personal gain. These men, women, and children had no rights and no reasonable hope of freedom. Slave owners could be cruel without any fear of backlash from the government or peers. Slaves were property at the mercy of their owners.

This practice of slavery, however, was not what slavery looked like in biblical times. Slavery has been around since almost the beginning of time, but its purpose and function in society as a whole differed greatly in New Testament times than it did in eighteenth- and nineteenth-century America.

First, in the Greco-Roman world of the New Testament (the culture and time surrounding the letter to Titus) slavery was not characterized by specific races or cultures. While American slaves were a different race than their masters, "most slaves in the Roman Empire were of the same race as their masters. Thus, most could not be identified as slaves on sight."[10] American slaves also differed from their masters in language, religion, culture, and values. They basically held nothing in common with their masters except being humans, though some slave masters even argued that point. Slaves in New Testament times, however, often shared language, religion, culture, and values with their owners.[11] While they were not peers in social status, Greco-Roman slaves were equal to their masters in many other areas, which was pretty much unheard of with American slaves. Jews were held to even higher standards by God's decree and were commanded, among other things, not to "rule with severity over one another."[12]

Second, the attitude toward slaves differed immensely between American and Greco-Roman cultures. A large majority of Americans viewed slaves as sub-human. They were denied education and only a select few were trusted with anything of value or importance to their masters. The Greco-Roman culture, however, viewed slaves equally as human beings. Slaves were not considered inferior at all, and thus were given much responsibility in high-level performing roles.[13]

Another major difference between these two slave cultures was the role of freedom. Generally speaking, American slaves were slaves for life unless they managed to escape (or were set free by their masters, which was rare). Contrarily, Greco-Roman slaves were often set free and could even earn their freedom. Many people sold themselves into slavery in order to pay off their debts, not worried one bit about attaining freedom once their debt was paid. Further, "freed slaves of Roman citizens typically received Roman citizenship," so someone could advance his social status simply by becoming a slave for a period of time.[14] Some slaves, once freed, even volunteered to remain servants for their master's family for the remainder of their lives.[15]

When Paul refers to himself as a **bond-servant of God**, therefore, he is not referring to himself as having zero worth, ready to be abused and despised by his master. Quite the opposite. He is a willing servant who longs to join himself to his Master, his Master's family (the church), and His work.

The other phrase Paul uses to describe himself is **an apostle of Jesus Christ**. While **bond-servant of God** alludes to Paul's posture before God and his commitment to advancing His mission on earth (as a slave would his master), **apostle to Jesus Christ** refers to "Paul's selection for service and his sending out by Christ himself. This is a technical designation of one to whom Christ's authority has been delegated."[16]

Jesus chose Paul specifically and spoke with him personally after His ascension to heaven. Even though eleven of Christ's disciples were still alive and actively advancing the gospel, Jesus chose Paul on the road to Damascus to bear His "name before the Gentiles and kings and the sons of Israel."[17] Paul served a designated role in the gospel's expansion on earth, and he identifies himself as **an apostle of Jesus Christ** as a reminder of that fact to those reading.

FOR THE FAITH OF THOSE CHOSEN OF GOD AND THE KNOWLEDGE OF THE TRUTH WHICH IS ACCORDING TO GODLINESS

This phrase describes Paul's apostleship, not the purpose of the book of Titus. Meaning, Paul's apostleship exists **for the faith of those chosen of**

God, and also exists for **the knowledge of the truth which is according to godliness.** Paul's goal as an apostle was the faith of believers, their knowledge of the truth, and their godliness.[18]

Faith is a familiar concept that's often misunderstood. We use it so frequently, it's kind of lost its meaning along the way. We have faith that good things will happen to us, faith in ourselves, faith in others, and of course, faith in God. But what is faith? As a primary purpose of Paul's life work (and imperative to our own salvation), it's worth a brief reminder.

The best definitions come straight from God. He gives us one in the book of Hebrews:

> "Now faith is the assurance of things hoped for, the conviction
> of things not seen … by faith we understand that the worlds were
> prepared by the word of God, so that what is seen was not made
> out of things which are visible."[19]

First and foremost, faith is confidence, particularly in God and His Word. Faith is not a wish. It's not something we want to happen but aren't entirely sure it will. That kind of perspective is the opposite of faith, for it puts no confidence in God at all.

Second, faith is a means. Faith in and of itself doesn't lead anywhere or accomplish anything. Rather, the object of our faith—who or what we put our faith in—gives faith substance and credit. As a crude example, we technically put faith in chairs when we sit in them. We don't question, doubt, or hesitate before sitting down for our morning tea and toast. We trust our chairs will hold us today, as they have for years. The concept translates to faith in God. When God is the object of our faith, we place confidence in the most reliable, steadfast, trustworthy being in the universe. We draw our assurance from Him, and faith is the means through which that occurs.

Finally for our discussion, faith gives perspective. In the passage above, we learn that faith gives us the ability to understand that the physical world isn't all there is. It was created by and for things not visible to the naked eye. In other words, faith enables us to trust God as our source and sustainer of life. He is working out everything for His glory and the good of those who love Him, even if we can't understand how it's all working out from what we see on earth.[20] Faith allows us to have confidence that this world—and all the messy, broken circumstances within it –is not our true home.

This is the genuine faith Paul strived to see realized in the hearts of people, specifically **those chosen of God.** Those who come to saving faith in Jesus Christ were predestined to do so since before the world was created.[21] This is neither the time nor place for a free will vs. predestination debate; for the purpose of this book and our discussion, it's enough to know that our faith in God is no accident. If you are saved (or desire to be), He has chosen you, ordained you, set you apart, and made you His own, all profound and extraordinary truths if you let your mind probe it.

Paul's apostleship exists to further **the faith of those chosen by God,** and also for their **knowledge of the truth that leads to godliness.** Faith in God cannot occur or mature without knowledge. The knowledge Paul refers to here is that of the gospel, for neither salvation nor sanctification can transpire without it.[22]

What is the gospel? It's literally good news. What good news? God's plan to rescue a spiritually dead, broken, condemned, and sin-enslaved world, giving eternal life and restoring it to peace with Him through the comprehensive and final sacrifice of Jesus Christ—who was born of a virgin, lived a sinless life, died on the cross, was buried, and rose again—bringing us to life in Him, adopting us into His family, and securing us in His glorious future.

In less eloquent terms, the gospel is God's rescue mission. He rescues people who can't even desire to be rescued (much less accomplish said rescue) on their own.

Knowing **the truth** of the gospel is the first step we take in receiving it. Once that knowledge has transformed into faith, it **leads to godliness** in our lives. Just as faith is a means to confidence and reliance upon God, knowledge is a means toward godliness in our lives.[23] Indeed, "it is those who know God's name who put their trust in Him."[24]

Knowledge on its own, however, does nothing but make us theologically fat. We may know a mountain of facts about the gospel, but if we don't exercise that knowledge (put it into practice) in our daily lives, it accomplishes nothing of eternal value. Paul's goal was not simply to inform people of the gospel, but to help them activate it—transforming their lives from depravity to godliness.

IN THE HOPE OF ETERNAL LIFE, WHICH GOD, WHO CANNOT LIE …

If the *goal* of Paul's apostleship is to further faith, knowledge, and godliness, then the *foundation* of his apostleship is **the hope of eternal life.** Our salvation (and every aspect of our spiritual lives and ministry) is built upon hope.

Hope is similar to faith in that it's a guaranteed expectation for believers, not a wish or fleeting desire for salvation to transpire. Some people consider themselves eternally safe because they're convinced that their good deeds outweigh their bad. They think that, when they meet Jesus face to face, He will let them enter heaven because their scale balances out enough to let them sneak on by. This assumption has many errors (including the gross lack of the gospel), but one somber error in this thinking is the absence of confidence. The overwhelming majority of people have zero confidence in their eternal destiny, despite yearning for it.

Jesus, on the other hand, offers absolute confidence in salvation. The hope He provides is based on who He is and what He has done for us. He gave up everything—left Heaven itself—to come to a miserably sin-infested world and died in order to save it. The salvation He offers is real, and we're to savor it with confidence from the moment we receive it.

Far too often in church circles, we think and talk of eternal life only in a future sense. While it's absolutely true that eternal life encompasses our future lives in heaven, it doesn't begin when we die. Rather, it begins the very moment we accept Jesus Christ as our personal Lord and Savior. One of Satan's greatest deceptions is swaying Christians to believe their eternal destinies begin when they die. By doing this, he robs us of the amazing life God wants us to experience now. Peace, hope, joy, love, faith, truth, patience, longsuffering, confidence, the very power of God Himself—all are accessible to believers now, through the Holy Spirit who dwells within us.

When we take full advantage of eternal life while still living on earth, we are empowered to deal with all of life's messiness and disappointments. If we're honest, life often isn't all that grand. Physical maladies, emotional scarring, relational failures, and hideous past experiences all serve to complicate our lives and make us yearn for heaven. But when we realize that, in one sense, heaven came with Jesus and remained with the Holy Spirit, we are able to tap into it now and receive the glorious, soul-rejuvenating benefits it offers. God doesn't want us to wait to experience life in Him. He wants us to experience Him in our current location on earth as well as our future location in heaven.

Our confidence in future glory increases exponentially when we live it out amidst the despair of this world. But just in case we fail or doubt (which we all do), Paul confirms our eternal security again by reminding us of its origin: God.

God, who cannot lie, promised eternal life. I love this. It would've been more than enough for Paul just to have written, "God promised long ages ago," because what God promises comes true. But Paul takes a step even further and reminds us that God **cannot lie**; thus, His promises have to come true. We're told one other place in the New Testament that God can't lie, and interestingly enough, it also comes in a passage about hope:

> In the same way God, desiring even more to show to the heirs of the promise the unchangeableness of His purpose, interposed with an oath, so that by two unchangeable things in which it is impossible for God to lie, we who have taken refuge would have strong encouragement to take hold of the hope set before us. This hope we have as an anchor of the soul, a hope both sure and steadfast ...[25]

God does not and cannot lie. He also does not change. Therefore, our hope in eternal life is 100 percent secure. It's the foundation we base our lives, faith, and pursuits on. Paul based his apostleship on this same hope.

While it's good to be reminded of God's utmost integrity, Paul has deeper motivations for reminding us that He cannot lie. We'll dig into background a bit more in the pages to come, but Paul is writing against a culture known for their ghastly lack of morals. To be more specific, these people were known throughout all the ancient world as liars.[26] Paul implements a bit of sarcasm and wit with this little reminder, then sets God starkly (and strategically) against the depravity of the targeted culture.

... PROMISED LONG AGES AGO, BUT AT THE PROPER TIME MANIFESTED, EVEN HIS WORD

One of my favorite characteristics to ponder about God is His infiniteness. He is limitless, immeasurable, unfathomable, countless. He's literally, figuratively, emotionally, (and every other kind of "ly" you can think of), too vast for us to comprehend.

An amazing aspect of His infiniteness is the fact that He exists outside of time. This truth makes my head hurt if I dwell on it too long, because, well, how nonsensical is that? He *created* time. He isn't bound by it in the least, though He operates within it for our benefit.

We understand little about time. Our whole lives are based on it and measured by it, but it also eludes us. We try to grasp its intangible hands but only find ourselves empty-handed from the effort.

Time affects all of us, but if we're in Christ, our souls are timeless in the best possible way. We are on earth for now, and our limited time here plays a part in the cosmic plan God's been unfolding since the beginning of creation. This cosmic plan is what Paul is writing about here. God promised eternal life **long ages ago.**

The first mention of the gospel is in Genesis 3, when God declares the punishment for Adam and Eve's disobedience. To the serpent, He said, "… I will put enmity between you and the woman, and between your seed and her seed; He shall bruise you on the head, and you shall bruise him on the heel."[27] The woman's seed is a direct reference to Christ, who would come and reverse the fall for mankind, bringing man to life in Him once more.

Promises of the Savior saturate the Old Testament, which spans more than a thousand years. Of course, God knew we would need the Gospel before He even created the world; hence, the **long ages ago.** He also knew the timing—when and how He would bring it about.

At the proper time God **manifested, even His word.** The world had to wait a long time for Jesus (i.e., the Word) to appear, and when He came,

He wasn't at all what people thought He would be. But God's plan was perfect, despite the world's poor reception. Consider this: Jesus came at a time when one empire controlled the majority of the world. That means that while most people were bilingual, most everyone knew a common language (Greek). The lack of language barrier allowed the gospel to spread like wildfire.

Additionally, Rome had developed road systems, making travel much easier. Ease of travel meant ease of carrying the gospel to various parts of the Roman empire—which is exactly what Paul did with his teams of missionaries. God manifested His Word in Christ, and Paul (and others) carried it forth to ignite the world with the gospel at the absolute perfect time in world history.

... IN THE PROCLAMATION WITH WHICH I WAS ENTRUSTED ACCORDING TO THE COMMANDMENT OF GOD OUR SAVIOR,

The proclamation Paul refers to here is that of the gospel. We are all supposed to preach the good news of Jesus Christ, but Paul had a special calling to do so as an **entrusted** agent by Christ Himself. As in other writings, "Paul consistently rooted his preaching in divine revelation rather than viewing it merely as a human message."[28]

With this statement, Paul brings it all back full circle. He began the introduction by proclaiming his identity as **a bond-servant of God and an apostle of Jesus Christ**, then explained the goal and foundation of his calling **for the faith of those chosen of God and the knowledge of the truth which is according to godliness.** Now he affirms "his authority as the one entrusted with the task of proclaiming the gospel."[29] His identity and calling were one and the same—deeply rooted in Christ and His gospel—and with it came influence and respect among the church, then and now.

TO TITUS, MY TRUE CHILD IN A COMMON FAITH:

Part of Paul's ministry philosophy involved training younger men to follow in his footsteps. Like other wise leaders, he realized he wouldn't live forever. He wanted his successors to carry on the work he began—along with finding their unique identity and calling in Christ and the advancement of His gospel. One such successor is the recipient of our book (and also its namesake): Titus. We don't know nearly as much about Titus as we do about his mentor, but he's not completely a mystery. While references about him are brief, we do learn enough to get a solid understanding of who this man was.

First, Titus was close to Paul. So close that Paul refers to him as his brother, partner, fellow worker, and **true child**.[30] Considering what we've briefly discussed about Paul, these are quite the compliments. Can you imagine being that dear to the apostle Paul? To spend countless hours with him as he ministered to people, traveled the known world to share God's truth, combated erroneous theology with gusto, inspired people to holy living, and lived in a closeness to God that can hardly be fathomed by the majority of evangelicals today? Not only that, but to discuss theology and ecclesiology at will, ask questions freely, pray with him, soak up wisdom from his experiences and faith, and be like family to him? That's enough to get my blood pumping, and Titus had all of it and more.

Being called his **true child in a common faith** is revealing too. It's one thing to be a prized employee or partner, but when a relationship bound by a common purpose becomes personal, it can be stronger than a blood tie. For Paul and Titus, it was exactly that. To our knowledge, Paul didn't have any biological children, so for Titus to fill that role (and perhaps even more greatly because of their common life work), meant immense love and fierce commitment from Paul. Paul loved Titus as he would his own child and was devoted to him personally and also to his ministry, which is both amazing and telling of Titus' character.

Titus was a solid man of God on his own merit. The apostle Paul didn't partner with people who were indifferent, lazy, dissentious, or apathetic to the gospel. Frankly, he avoided people like that, shaking the dust off his feet to those who rejected the truth after hearing it.[31] So for him to have partnered with and mentored Titus is a huge tell in itself.

Certain hints throughout Paul's letters testify to Titus' character: his presence was comforting (2 Corinthians 7:6), he was full of joy and refreshed by other believers (2 Corinthians 7:13), he was earnest on behalf of others (2 Corinthians 8:16), he did not take advantage of people or situations (2 Corinthians 12:18), he did not cave to pressure of the Jews (Galatians 2:3), and he went where he was needed (2 Timothy 4:10). Titus was a man who lived righteously and served hard—putting the spread of the gospel before his comfort and convenience. His inner strength and commitment to the gospel made him a man worth looking up to. Paul saw a spark in him that was worth the countless hours, prayer, and personal investment needed to fan it into flame.

Titus was also Greek. This is interesting because 1) Greeks (and Gentiles in general) were new to the faith, and 2) Titus opted not to convert to Judaic laws in order to pursue his faith in Christ. Let's back up a little to put this into context. From the beginning, God chose Israel to be the people who would proclaim Him to the rest of the world.[32] Thus, anyone who wanted to be saved had to convert to Judaism and adhere to all its laws—circumcision, sacrifices, feasts, tithes, and all.

Unfortunately, the Jews did not do their job very well, and in many ways they became a hindrance to the gospel instead of a propellant. Rather than sharing God with the world, they muted Him by contaminating the laws He gave them (adding several hundred, which made them self-righteous and arrogant). When they weren't obsessing over religious duties and obligations, they were ignoring Him completely and prostituting themselves to other nations and their religions. It's not surprising, then, that they completely misread the identity of Jesus when He arrived. Jesus preached the heart of the Law they had missed entirely; and because He threatened their egos (among other things), they despised and ultimately crucified Him.

Fast forward to Titus' day. The early believers (including the apostle Peter) thought they were still Jews, that the gospel was merely the continuation of the religion they'd held before Christ arrived. Thus, they initially required people to convert to Judaism in order to receive salvation and the Holy Spirit. God combatted this mistake of Peter's early on, but it was still tough for the apostles and disciples to thoroughly embrace.[33] Paul fought aggressively for the unconditional inclusion of Gentiles into the faith, and Titus exemplified his agenda. Titus did not get circumcised (a tremendous moment of personal relief, I'm sure!) when he came to faith in Christ, thus he did not convert to Judaism. God accepted him just as He did converted Jews, validating the point that Christ came for *all* who would call upon the name of the Lord and be saved, both Jew and Gentile.[34]

We may not be given a ton of information about Titus, but we can responsibly deduce much from what we have. As Paul's mentee, he played a vital role in the establishment of the church, served as a prominent member of the faith in his own merit, and stood as an example, validating the inclusion of Gentiles into the faith without first converting to Judaism.

A QUICK NOTE ABOUT GENRE

One note we must explore before we move on is the genre or category of the book of Titus. As the introduction has led us to observe, there is an author and recipient, making the book of Titus personal communication—a letter between two comrades in the faith. In this case, the book of Titus is also one of three pastoral letters that were written from a pastor to individual mentees who also served as pastors (not written to whole church communities).[35]

One beautiful thing about the Bible is its diversity, specifically in literary styles. God could've easily given us a strict list of rules and left us on our own to make sense of it and life. For that matter, He could've left us without anything at all and would have been completely justified doing so. But he didn't. He gave us an intricate, bottomless wealth of truth delivered via sixty books comprising one large one.

Part of His creativity is shown in the genres that make up His Word. We are given historical narratives, wisdom literature, poetry, prophetic literature, gospels, and our focus—letters. The letters are found in the New Testament and are exactly what their names suggest: letters written from an individual to another individual or group.

Letter writing is a dying form nowadays, but let's put on our nostalgic glasses and remember what they used to be: snail mail. Since the time humanity created alphabets and established the craft of writing, people have written letters to one another. (Still do, but in abbreviated, electronic forms.) The book of Titus is such a letter, from the apostle Paul to one of his protégés, Titus.

While this all may seem obvious, exploring the concept of letters will help us identify with the book of Titus even more. First to remember, letters back then were hand-written and hand-delivered to specific people. In other words, they were incredibly intentional. They took thought, energy, and a lot of time—both to write and then deliver.

Second, they were also considered authoritative. Letters (and the instruction they contained) were accepted as direct extensions of their authors. Thus, individuals and churches who received letters from apostles understood the content was not to be taken lightly. Receiving a letter was synonymous with receiving the apostle who wrote it, and their words were highly esteemed.

Third, while letters were read by the individuals to whom they were addressed, letters written to churches were read aloud to their congregants. Church buildings didn't exist back then; letters were passed around from house church to house church until they all heard the message. The letter to Titus was first personal, but as we will see, it definitely contains instruction for the Titus' church as well.

Lastly, letters were contextual. They address specific people in a specific place at a specific time for a specific purpose. We're amiss to think we can read and directly apply a New Testament letter as if God is writing directly to us. He isn't. He wrote through the apostles in specific circumstances to communicate timeless theological truths that we first glean *and then* apply to our lives. We absolutely must keep letters (along with every other genre in Scripture) within their specific context. Otherwise, we run the risk of mishandling God's Word—a prospect believers shudder at and demons rejoice over because of the devastating consequences it can wreak within the church.

Genre is far from trivial when studying a book of the Bible. It allows us to place this particular part of Scripture within the context it was inspired, written, and ordained for. Then we can, in turn, handle it appropriately as we apply it to our lives. In the book of Titus, we read personal correspondence between two men whom we greatly respect and admire. We get a glimpse into their relationship and circumstances, as well as what was happening on the ministry front where they were each based. Keeping this in mind as we continue our journey will help bring a strict, one-dimensional view of this letter to a full, three-dimensional experience of it.

GRACE AND PEACE FROM GOD THE FATHER AND CHRIST JESUS OUR SAVIOR.

Paul began and concluded many of his letters with a blessing like **grace and peace from God the Father and Christ Jesus our Savior.** To be thorough, this is the only time this phrase is worded exactly this way in the

New Testament letters. Many times he writes, "grace to you and peace from God our Father and the Lord Jesus Christ," but the point remains.[36] Paul's blessing and prayer is for the recipient(s), in this case, Titus, to experience fully the **grace and peace** from his letter and in general.

Grace, like faith, is a term used so frequently in church circles, it's almost lost its meaning. Or at least, its full effect upon reading or hearing it. It means the full, "unmerited favor of God toward fallen man whereby, for the sake of Christ—the only begotten of the Father, full of grace and truth (John 1:14)—he has provided for man's redemption."[37] So yes, it's kind of a big deal.

Going back to the gospel and the reason we need it in the first place, mankind is dead—in a spiritual state of decay without even a semblance of a heartbeat—before God divinely intervenes and shocks us to life in Christ. This act is, in part, grace. The only things we deserve are the hell, fire, and brimstone old-school preachers love to harp on. We deserve to be left in our own pits of self-destruction without any hope of rescue or life. But God chose grace. He looked upon us with unmerited favor and sent Christ to take the punishment for our sins so He still can see us through a lens of unmerited favor.

One result of this unmerited favor is peace, both with God and from God. This is also a big deal.
The metaphor of being dead before Christ may mislead us to think we're in a neutral standing with Him, since dead is rather dormant. Quite the contrary. Instead of being in His favor, we are the objects of His wrath and would be for eternity if He hadn't intervened. Being at peace with God, then, is quite the envious position.

But we also receive peace *from* God, and this is what Paul refers to in his greeting to Titus. Salvation brings peace to our very souls—"the peace of God, which surpasses all comprehension, will guard your hearts and your minds in Christ Jesus."[38] Because of Christ, we can access deep peace, regardless of any turbulent circumstances shaking up our lives. This peace, to Titus and any other ministry worker during this time, would be refreshing indeed, because of the particularly strenuous nature of their calling.

While grace and peace remain individual entities, they are two facets of the endless prism of salvation that work together to draw sustenance for the believer. When believers "become absolutely convinced that their standing before God is based entirely on his grace and not on any goodness in themselves, peace comes," and both grace and peace remain because the Holy Spirit does as well.[39]

Being a recipient of God's grace and peace is nothing short of a miracle. No one deserves them. No one can earn them. But a wise soul will recognize these gifts and receive them with an eager heart. Also, we can keep receiving grace and peace. God extends them to us at the initial point of salvation, sure, but Paul communicates in his letters that we can grasp grace and peace repeatedly throughout our faith journeys.

Paul extends this greeting of blessing with paramount fervor. He stands confident in his identity in Christ as a bond-servant and apostle for the purpose of furthering the faith, knowledge, and godliness of believers in the hope of eternal life. All this, of course, is built upon the foundation of the gospel God has worked throughout history, of which Paul has been ordained an agent. Titus, a spiritual son to Paul and an admirable man in his own right, also received a calling to cultivate the gospel in hearts throughout the world. He receives this letter and powerful greeting from his mentor for continued grace and peace in God as he goes about his gospel work.

GROUP STUDY

INTRODUCTION

> Identity is a life that awaits, rather than an object to be found.

The term identity is a bit misleading, because our identity is never found on its own, but rather in something or someone else. As much as we think otherwise, we are not autonomous beings. We greatly depend on things outside ourselves to find answers to life, meaning, and purpose.

- What are some things our culture wants us to place our identity in?
- Share one or two things you've erroneously placed your identity in before.

THE WORD

The introduction to Paul's letter to Titus contains an inspiring worldview of identity. Paul knows who he is and is well aware of how that identity unfolds in his daily life:

> Paul, a bond-servant of God and an apostle of Jesus Christ, for the faith of those chosen of God and the knowledge of the truth which is according to godliness, in the hope of eternal life, which God, who cannot lie, promised long ages ago, but at the proper time manifested, even His word, in the proclamation with which I was entrusted according to the commandment of God our Savior, to Titus, my true child in a common faith: Grace and peace from God the Father and Christ Jesus our Savior. (Titus 1:1-4)

- What two phrases does Paul use right away to describe himself?

  - Why do you think it's difficult for people to identify with the first?

- Paul's identity in Christ informs his life purpose and goals thereof, which he describes as:

  … for the _____ of those chosen of God

  and the _____ of the truth

  which is according to _____.

  - What is the relationship among these three purposes?

- These purposes are grounded in a promise. What did God promise long ages ago?

  The _____ of _____ _____.

  - Why is that promise important?

APPLY

Our identities are inextricably linked to our purpose here on earth, neither of which can be realized apart from God through Christ.

> Therefore if anyone is in Christ, he is a new creature;
> The old things passed away; behold, new things have come.
> The Apostle Paul, 2 Corinthians 5:17

> Man's chief end is to glorify God, and to enjoy Him forever.
> Westminster Shorter Catechism

When we receive Christ as our personal Lord and Savior, we become new people. Christianity is not a cloak we put on top of our old selves, nor is it an accessory we add to the ensemble of our souls. Rather, it's a strip-naked-before-God-in-all-our-shame, get-cleansed-from-the-inside-out, receive-new-heavenly-garmets-to-hold-us-over-until-we-get-new-heavenly-bodies kind of experience.

At the same time, we are transformed completely (in our status before God) and enter into the process of transformation (sanctification) that will carry on through heaven. Our identities are secure in Christ and are continually being molded into His image as we increase in our faith, knowledge of the truth, and godliness.

Our identity is Christ, and our purpose is to glorify God and enjoy Him forever. Paul (and Titus) did this exceedingly well. He gave his life to the advancement of the gospel in others' lives. While it wasn't all daisies and roses (in his case, more like chains, beatings, and shipwrecks), he pursued this purpose with a passion that still inspires millions of believers today.

- What is presently trying to compete with Christ as the securer of your identity? Or, what parts of your "old creature" still have a death grip on your life?

- List three distractions that hinder you from fulling your purpose: to glorify God and enjoy Him forever.

  - _____
  - _____
  - _____

- What is ONE practical step you can take this week to live out the reality of who you are in Christ?

WEEK TWO
TITUS 1:5-16

PERSONAL BIBLE STUDY QUESTIONS

1. Why did Paul leave Titus in Crete? (1:5)

2. What are the qualifications of an elder/overseer? (1:6-9)

    a)

    b)

    c)

    d)

    e)

    f)

    g)

    h)

    i)

    j)

k)

l)

m)

n)

o)

p)

q)

r)

s)

t)

3. Immediately after discussing elder qualifications, Paul warns Timothy of a group of people. Who are they? (1:10)

    a) Why are they so dangerous? (1:11)

4. Why was Titus told to reprove the Cretans severely? (1:13)

5. Why do actions matter just as much as (or perhaps more than) words? (1:16)

COMMENTARY

For this reason I left you in Crete, that you would set in order what remains and appoint elders in every city as I directed you, namely, if any man is above reproach, the husband of one wife, having children who believe, not accused of dissipation or rebellion. For the overseer must be above reproach as God's steward, not self-willed, not quick-tempered, not addicted to wine, not pugnacious, not fond of sordid gain, but hospitable, loving what is good, sensible, just, devout, self-controlled, holding fast the faithful word which is in accordance with the teaching, so that he will be able both to exhort in sound doctrine and to refute those who contradict. For there are many rebellious men, empty talkers and deceivers, especially those of the circumcision, who must be silenced because they are upsetting whole families, teaching things they should not teach for the sake of sordid gain. One of themselves, a prophet of their own said, "Cretans are always liars, evil beasts, lazy gluttons." This testimony is true. For this reason reprove them severely so that they may be sound in the faith, not paying attention to Jewish myths and commandments of men who turn away from the truth. To the pure, all things are pure; but to those who are defiled and unbelieving, nothing is pure, but both their mind and their conscience are defiled. They profess to know God, but by their deeds they deny Him, being detestable and disobedient and worthless for any good deed.

Titus 1:5-16

Leadership exists in families, organizations, businesses, governments, and world powers. We need leaders for several reasons—to create and enforce guidelines that keep society functioning well, to inspire us, to empower us to reach our fullest potential, to keep us looking ahead, to remind us where we come from, to support us when we face roadblocks, to work out kinks in the system, and to bring us together for a common goal.

Great leaders accomplish this with diligence and poise, making it effortless for people to follow. Poor leaders cause dissention, rebellion, chaos, and bitterness among their subjects. While we don't always get to choose the quality of our leadership, we do realize leaders are necessary. We do everything within our power to install leaders we want to follow.

As a major leader of the church, Paul understood what was required of a leader, especially a Christian one. His mantra for leadership was flawless. "Be imitators of me, just as I also am of Christ."[40] He understood that he led people only where he went first: straight to Jesus Christ. He invested a lot of time, energy, and prayer into others' leadership abilities (like Titus') as well, and this passage provides us with foundational character traits of people qualified to serve as Christian leaders within the church.

FOR THIS REASON I LEFT YOU IN CRETE, THAT YOU WOULD SET IN ORDER WHAT REMAINS AND APPOINT ELDERS IN EVERY CITY AS I DIRECTED YOU

We now obtain insight into the context surrounding Paul's letter to Titus. On a previous journey, he and Titus had visited Crete and begun a church there. Since Crete didn't have a spiritually mature enough presence for the church to thrive on its own, Paul left Titus to carry out the task—to **set in order what remains and appoint elders in every city as I directed.** But before we dig into all the task would entail, let's back up and explore the origin of the Cretan church a bit more.

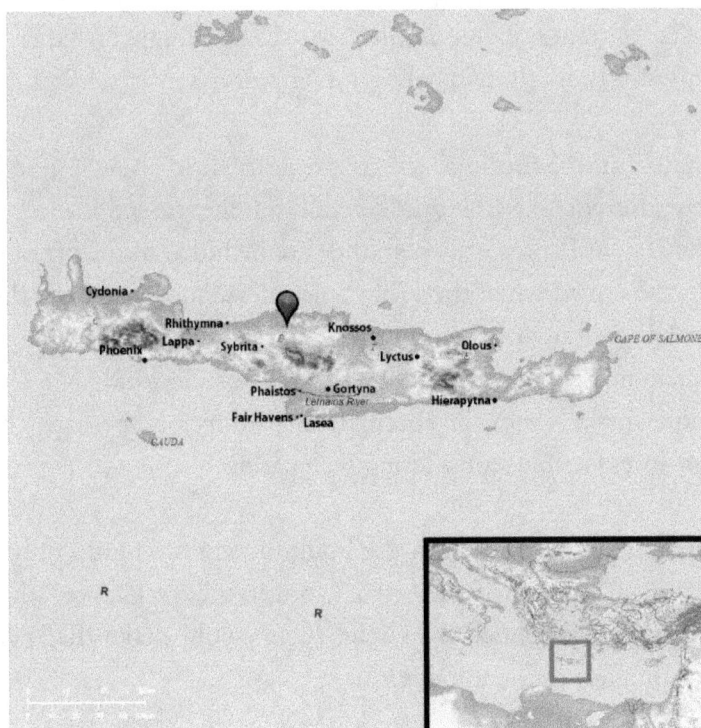

Map accredited to Biblos.com

Crete (now Candia) was a relatively large island located in the Mediterranean Sea. It stands 156 miles long and ranges from 7 to 30 miles across, with a mountain in the middle that reaches over 8,000 feet.[41] Its strategic location made it indispensable for sea trade, and it also served as a weigh station for said trade.[42] In the ancient world, it was a great center of business, though it "never attained a prominent place in history" due to a gross lack of morals displayed by its inhabitants.[43] But what it lacked in morals it made up for in convenience, a "one-stop shop" of sorts. Not only was it a desirable location for commerce, like any other major trade location in that day, it was also "a place where most of the current philosophies and religions would pass through at one point or another, undoubtedly leaving their marks."[44] This made it a desirable location for the gospel to be shared, for a church there would ensure major evangelization to the vast number of businessmen who came through.

Despite its horrendous reputation for base morals, it was full of opportunity for those shrewd enough to envision it.

Unfortunately, the Scriptures tell us precious little about Crete and its subsequent church. The first time Cretans are mentioned is in Acts 2:11, during the Day of Pentecost, where they are included in the list of nations present in the crowd when the Holy Spirit descended upon the disciples. We don't know if any of them received Christ that day, but it's possible some of them made it back to Crete with at least some kind of gossip about such a noteworthy event. A speculative assumption, perhaps, but not altogether unreasonable, considering its location.

Other mentions of Crete within the book of Acts are found only during the story of Paul's shipwreck in Acts 27. But in these references, there's no indication they ever landed on Crete, so it would make that particular experience unlikely as the initial visit.

Other than that, Scripture is silent about the island of Crete. While we may want to know more, it's profound that a center of ministry as strategic as Crete remains unspoken of, for it reveals an interesting truth about God's work and the Bible's articulation of it—a lot more happened during that time than what we're told in Scripture. (And Scripture tells us a great deal). God's presence and movement in the world cannot be contained in a single book. The Apostle John confirms this thought in his gospel letter when writing about Jesus' ministry:

> This is the disciple who is testifying to these things and wrote these things, and we know that his testimony is true. And there are also many other things which Jesus did, which if they were written in detail, I suppose that even the world itself would not contain the books that would be written.[45]

If the entire world wouldn't be big enough to contain books written about Jesus' life and ministry, there's not a chance it'd be big enough to contain every single way God moved in the world during the beginning of the church. It's reassuring, then, that Crete remains rather mysterious. It reminds us that God is doing far more than we are capable of realizing. What we do know about Crete is enough: that it was chosen by Paul as a strategic location to establish a church, and that he deemed Titus worthy of such a task.

Titus's commission in Crete was two-fold—**to set in order what remains** and also to **appoint elders in every city**, as Paul had previously directed him to do. **To set in order what remains** is rather vague, but we will see hints as we continue to move throughout the letter. (Remember, nothing was vague to Titus as the recipient of the letter, for he knew and worked with Paul closely in life as well as on this particular mission).

To appoint elders in every city was standard practice for Paul in his efforts to establish churches in new geographical locations.[46] Again, the church was just beginning at this time in history. It was a brand-new religion in that Jesus broke the chains of the law that had bound Jews for centuries, and that He embraced all people, despite previous religion, race, or status. Because of that, church buildings as we know them didn't exist. In fact, the structure of the church doesn't look much at all like we're used to seeing, with myriads of church buildings to choose from on any given weekend.

Rather, churches were largely house churches. Paul (or another apostle or disciple) would enter a new location (city, town, village, etc.), share the gospel, and lead a number of people to Christ. He'd remain for a time (or leave one of his protégés) to disciple the new believers and establish a church, then he would move on and repeat the process. He would return to visit when he could, and/or would write letters, encouraging them and combatting any erroneous doctrine he'd heard they were struggling with.

By and large, churches met in individual families' homes, not independent building structures. As they grew, the number of home churches increased to sustain the growth. Because of this, single lead pastors like we have in most churches today weren't necessary. Rather, early churches instituted elders and other forms of church leadership to lead the house congregations and to remain in communication with the apostles via letters and visits.

Titus was left in Crete for that exact mission—to establish Cretan congregations in their doctrine and lifestyles by securing leadership who would hold them accountable and inspire them to follow suit. Since Crete was a rather large island with many cities, this was no small task, which confirms Titus' character and competence once again.

Yet it also reveals Paul's rather brilliant leadership philosophy. While Paul tells Titus *what* he must do (**as I directed you**), he leaves the *how* up to him. Quite an ingenious display of empowered leadership. Rather than micromanaging or demanding specific directions be followed (poor leadership), Paul trusts Titus, allowing him creative freedom in bringing his task to life, and offers full support (excellent leadership). Despite being one of the most mightily used men in the establishment of the church, Paul wasn't a control freak. He kept the mission of the gospel in the forefront of his mind and trusted that the same Spirit who empowered him would also empower those he trained to accomplish amazing things for the kingdom of God.

Titus' task in Crete is extensive, but he's authorized and able to do it, first by the Holy Spirit and then by a great mentor like Paul. The letter in itself serves as a substantial tool of confidence, reminding Titus who they both are in Christ, reinforcing the mission, and offering authoritative support Titus can lean on and measure his work against.

NAMELY, IF ANY MAN IS ABOVE REPROACH, THE HUSBAND OF ONE WIFE, HAVING CHILDREN WHO BELIEVE, NOT ACCUSED OF DISSIPATION OR REBELLION. FOR THE OVERSEER MUST BE ABOVE

REPROACH AS GOD'S STEWARD, NOT SELF-WILLED, NOT QUICK-TEMPERED, NOT ADDICTED TO WINE, NOT PUGNACIOUS, NOT FOND OF SORDID GAIN, BUT HOSPITABLE, LOVING WHAT IS GOOD, SENSIBLE, JUST, DEVOUT, SELF-CONTROLLED, HOLDING FAST THE FAITHFUL WORD WHICH IS IN ACCORDANCE WITH THE TEACHING, SO THAT HE WILL BE ABLE BOTH TO EXHORT IN SOUND DOCTRINE AND TO REFUTE THOSE WHO CONTRADICT.

Begin your celebration, Type A friends; we now encounter our first list. Paul supplies Titus with a list of character traits used to measure the viability of elder candidates.[47] The terms **elder** and **overseer** are used synonymously in this letter (and elsewhere throughout the New Testament), and they were the primary form of leadership within individual house church congregations. Again, single or lead pastors as we know them today didn't exist, nor did an official process of established ordination. (That practice came along in the beginning of the second century).[48] Elders, then, were appointed by apostles and their delegates and confirmed by their individual congregations for the purpose of teaching and caring for the people in their charge.[49]

Because of the weighty position of spiritual authority, it was imperative to find men who embodied numerous character traits considered worthy of their calling. Each of these traits could be the subject matter of an entire book, but a brief polish individually will give us a cohesive view of the ideal man for this position.

Qualifications of an Elder:

- Man
- Above reproach
- Husband of one wife
- Have children who believe
- Not accused of dissipation

- Not accused of rebellion
- Above reproach as God's steward
- Not self-willed
- Not quick-tempered
- Not addicted to wine
- Not pugnacious
- Not fond of sordid gain
- Hospitable
- Loving what is good
- Sensible
- Just
- Devout
- Self-controlled
- Holding fast the faithful word

First, only men were permitted to be elders. I know, I know; dicey subject. Without getting completely sidetracked from our intended purpose, we'll explore a few facts about gender distinction that will help us gain a more complete picture of what God intended for an elder.

Foremost, male headship is not an affront to women. It is a specific and deliberate design by God Himself that began when He created the world. God created men and women one-hundred percent equal in value, significance, and worth. A one hundred dollar bill is worth the exact same as a one hundred dollar check. But having the same worth does not mean they are composed the same, nor do they have identical functions. Likewise, men and women are equal in value, different in design.

Amongst other things, God created men as protectors and providers. They find great fulfillment in securing, serving, and providing for their families' needs and desires. Even their physiques and emotions attest to this. Men are physically strong, tend to be more stoic in their emotions, and think in a linear fashion.

Women, on the other hand, are created as powerful counterparts to their male equals. They possess a gentle grace (that seems to elude the male population), harness great emotion that makes them acutely relational, and think in a labyrinth capacity that enables them to see the forest *and* individual trees at the same time.

These are generalities, of course, but the point remains: men and women are equal in worth and yet different in design. God designed them to complement one another, to balance each other's strengths and weaknesses as both work for a common goal. God thought it best to appoint men into the position of eldership within the church, as it best complemented the gender roles He originally established in Eden. Women also held leadership roles within the church, and some were even established as deaconesses, but the specific role of elder remained for men (more male headship discussion to come in chapter three).

Gender is a fairly straightforward qualifier to suggest eligibility, but not so much the first character trait: elder candidates had to be **above reproach.** In Greek, this term is *anegkletos* and means not to be accused, to be blameless in reputation.[50] This qualification could easily stand alone, for it encompasses all the others and touches on every facet of an individual's life—spiritually, relationally, emotionally, in professional circles, in the home, etc. People who are **above reproach** have unshakable reputations built over years of consistent integrity.

Such reputations are earned via the personal and professional relationships elder candidates have with others. In order for an elder, then, to have been above reproach in his reputation, he first would've had to be known. Seems like a fairly obvious observation, but think about it. He was a man involved in and committed to relationships. He wasn't a hermit; rather, he invested in the lives of those around him.

Cultures change, but people don't. Relationships are messy because people are. While it may be easier to keep people at a distance, an elder chose to be involved in the lives of those around him. People knew him, knew of him, and knew there was something different—something good—about him, especially in light of the loathsome Cretan culture.

Those who knew him also must have held him in high esteem. His interactions with everyone from his family to random strangers must've been intentionally and consistently positive. Reputations aren't built overnight; they're established over years of steady, reliable behavior in any and every circumstance and relationship. That's not to say an elder never erred. Rather, when he did, he handled his blunder with humility and accepted consequences with integrity.

This character trait is one of the first things that attracted me to my husband when we met. He was (and is) consistent—in all his relationships and in every circumstance. It doesn't matter if he's with me on a date or at work negotiating with a difficult client, his attitude, demeanor, and conduct is genuine, godly, and consistent. He doesn't put on a mask or try to impress people with a different version of himself that changes with circumstances. He interacts with CEOs the same way he does with a waiter at a restaurant, and that kind of integrity draws people to him and, more importantly, to the God he loves.

That's the kind of man Titus was looking for in an elder for the Cretan church. He desired men who had solid reputations both personally and professionally, being known and esteemed within their homes and communities alike.

From here on in our passage, the **above reproach** factor is broken down into three categories that each contain specific areas in which an elder must be blameless: his family, his character, and his commitment to ministry within the church.[51]

The family category contains instructions about his marriage and children, because Paul wisely recognizes that "Christianity begins at home ... all the church service in the world will not make amends for neglect of a church official's family."[52] In the hierarchy of priorities, it's God first, family second. Everything else, in varying degrees, follows those two. Work or service always comes after family, so it's no surprise Paul begins with family in the breakdown of elder qualifications.

Regarding marriage, elders must be **the husband of one wife.** Many people raise their eyebrows at this because it seems to suggest that elders had to be married or could be married only once. This would disqualify divorced or widowed and remarried men. However, when digging into the Greek text, we find this phrase "describes fidelity within marriage and does not specifically delve into matters of polygamy or remarriage."[53] Thus, a man must be faithful to the wife he has—if he has one—to be considered as an elder.

The next two family instructions regard children: he must have **children who believe,** and children who are **not accused of dissipation or rebellion.** This seems like a tall order because to what degree and for how long can we be reasonably responsible for the actions and beliefs of our children? We all know awesome parents with kids who have strayed, just as we know horrible parents who have kids who rise above and become poster children for Christianity everywhere. Does Paul mean this as it sounds at first glance? Yes and no.

Once again, the original context is crucial for understanding it properly. The word **believe** in Greek (*pistos*) holds a number of possible definitions that must be analyzed within the usage and framework of its specific context. It can be translated as trusting faithful, easily persuaded, believing, or even steady and stable.[54] Analyzing our passage on its own, as well as within the context of other pastoral letters, we can reasonably conclude that **believe** means to have faith in God.[55] A crucial caveat to note, however, is that of time. It's most likely Paul is speaking of children who are still minors, living at home, and directly under their parents' authority—not adults.[56] With this in mind, Paul's logic is simple: parents can't expect to lead God's family if they've failed leading their own, just as they cannot expect to win strangers to Christ if they've failed to inspire their family members to do so as well.[57]

This logic continues with the mandate that elders must have children who are **not accused of dissipation or rebellion.** On an island characterized by the horrendous depravity of its inhabitants, Paul calls for a stark difference in the families of those leading the church. Lives of Christians must stand out in a surrounding world of darkness, for we are carriers of God's light.[58] Elders were men called to shine God's light personally, professionally, in their marriages, and with their children. Since family life is the most important calling in life after accepting Christ, elders had to show their commitment to family before being considered for a greater commitment to the church.

Having proven his **above-reproach** character in his family, an elder next must be **above reproach** in the realm of his character or personality, described in both negative traits to avoid and positive traits to embrace. To make sure Titus (and anyone else who would eventually read this letter), understands the point, Paul repeats that **the overseer must be above reproach**, this time adding **as God's steward.** Stewardship is a familiar concept in New Testament letters, both in reference to church leadership and Christians in general. Stewards are managers, keepers, and overseers of whatever has been assigned to their care. For the Cretan church, elders must be blameless stewards, not just for their families (and personal life), but for the church congregations in their charge. In other words, they must recognize their position as an extension of God's authority, not of their own, and let that perspective drive their actions.

Most of us will never serve as elders, but we are all stewards if we are in Christ. This perspective is tremendously helpful for faith in general and daily life specifically. Contrary to what culture would have us believe, we own nothing—not our homes, cars, or even the clothes on our back. Rather, all the physical (or nonphysical, for that matter) items within our possession are gifts given to us for a season determined by God Himself. Remember Job? He was extremely wealthy and "owned" more than we'll ever dream of, this side of heaven. But he understood that he was merely a steward of gifts God had given him. When God decided to take them away, Job still praised God:

> Naked I came from my mother's womb
> And naked I shall return there.
> The Lord gave and the Lord has taken away.
> Blessed be the name of the Lord.[59]

Knowing he was a steward instead of an owner allowed Job to live with open hands, receiving God's blessings but not hoarding them. We are wise to adopt such a perspective and will experience much more peace and joy if we do. Elder candidates had to embrace this ideology as well, allowing it to impact their view of their lives and their authority within the church.

Once understanding that he is but a steward of God's possessions, an elder must not be **self-willed.** The root of this word means "a fundamental selfishness that compels one to ride roughshod over others in the effort to satisfy oneself."[60] Such behavior was standard in Crete and the blatant antithesis of God and what He calls for in His servants.

Men who were **self-willed** prioritized themselves and worldly pursuits over and above anyone or anything else. If they desired wealth, they did everything they could to get it. They'd cast family, friends, even morals aside to acquire the financial security they wanted. An elder, contrarily, was a man who submitted his desires to the gospel—God first, family second, and church third. He didn't chase after the empty pursuits of this world, but rather allowed God to determine his endeavors. His concern was for others first. His life and undertakings therein reflected that.

Typically, selfless men were also not **quick-tempered.** Quick-tempered refers to uncontrolled anger, not anger in itself. Anger alone is not a sin. In fact, elsewhere Paul tells believers to "be angry, and yet do not sin; do not let the sun go down on your anger, and do not give the devil an opportunity."[61] This world is full of atrocities that should make us angry: abuse, neglect, murder, injustice, etc. Even Jesus became angry.

Our response to anger is the issue here. Elders (like any other man in authority) dealt with the messiness of people's lives. They would've inevitably become angry and impatient. But those qualified for the position of elder knew how to manage their responses to anger and control their emotions. They kept level heads so they could evaluate situations objectively and make decisions based on the gospel perspective, not one clouded with their tempers.

Part of a blameless character is also someone who is **not addicted to wine.** Alcohol can be a fierce topic in Christian circles. Some churches advocate strict abstinence while others permit its consumption freely (though responsibly). Nowhere in Scripture does God forbid the consumption of alcohol; thus, drinking it is not a sin. Believers are free to partake or abstain as they feel convicted on the matter, and judgment of others for their choices is not acceptable. While partaking of alcohol is not sinful, drunkenness and addiction are. Addiction is the main issue of concern in regard to eldership in the Cretan church. As with anger, elders needed to exercise self-control with alcohol. They needed to control substances and emotions, not be controlled by them.

Pugnacious or violent is also an unacceptable character trait for those being considered for eldership. Violence can be a byproduct of the drunkenness and anger mentioned above, but it can also stand on its own and be executed both physically and verbally. No violence is tolerable for Christians, especially those rising into leadership positions. While fists or verbal barbs can silence disputes, they never resolve them, and they don't glorify God.

Paul sums up the list of the negative character traits with the instruction that elders must not be **fond of sordid gain.** This phrase is translated several ways among versions of the Bible: "not given to filthy lucre" (KJV), "not greedy for money" (NKJV), not "dishonest with money" (NLT), "not pursuing dishonest gain" (NIV), and not "greedy for gain" (ESV) are just some examples. All these translations encompass the core point: elders must be responsible in their pursuit and management of finances. Implications of this instruction are vast. Elders should be employed in a reputable manner, be thoroughly honest in financial transactions, both personal and with those involving the church; and are never to use "Christian service as an opportunity for financial profit."[62] The temptress of money allures many, but elders were to stand strong against any seduction of misuse.

Still within the category of character and personality, Paul now shifts from negative traits that shouldn't be present in elders to positive traits they should possess, beginning with elders being **hospitable.** Hospitality differs from culture to culture, age to age. In the Greco-Roman world, hospitality was a "virtue, but it was also a thoroughgoing expectation of all Christians in the early church."[63] Again, church buildings as we know them did not exist. Instead, Christians worshiped in the houses of the congregants, making hospitality a rather large component of services.[64] Elders had to operate with an open-door perspective, providing an available and secure space for church members when needed. Quantity or extravagance of space wasn't important; hospitable welcoming and attention were.

Elders also had to be men who loved **what is good.** This portrays a leader who valued relationships and endeavors that were righteous and honorable, over and above things that are trivial and eternally insignificant.[65] We choose our pursuits, and our choices are revealed in how we spend our time. Elders invested their time and pursuits wisely, operating from a kingdom perspective rather than a dimmed, dingy, Cretan one.

Loving what is good reveals a man's prudence. Elders need to be **sensible** and sober in their thinking, dealings, and relationships. Brash decisions and reckless chases make an awful, uninspiring leader. No one wants to follow someone whose emotions change with the wind. Elders, then, were men who were responsible in their thoughts and rationale, which led to cool-headedness in the situations they faced.

An unjust man is as difficult to follow as a foolhardy one. But a **just** man—someone who is upright and righteous[66]—is a man worth committing to, for he commits himself to God. Being **just** isn't always easy, especially when one has an easy (albeit erring) way out. But right is right, and it directly reflects the God we know, love, serve, and represent. Elders were committed to being upright, regardless of circumstance or trial.

A commitment to being just complements an elder's commitment to being **devout**. Many of the aforementioned characteristics are marked by deliberate choices over long periods of time. For example, not being self-willed requires deliberate choices to yield to the Holy Spirit rather than oneself. Not being quick-tempered demands one practice restraining emotions on a continual basis until the temper is no longer easily triggered. Other characteristics follow the same logic; devoutness (or holiness) is no different. Being devout is a practice—a repeated exercise of faithfulness to God made up of deliberate choices, day in and day out, to do just that.

Self-controlled ends the list of traits in the character or personality category. It also means disciplined and carries with it the idea of being "in full control of oneself (one's temper, moods, behavior, and so on). This observable quality is truly a mark of the Spirit's work in an individual."[67] Discipline is not a popular concept in a world smitten with a do-whatever-makes-you-feel-good worldview. But those who exercise discipline—especially when done with solid motivations—please God and shine His light a little brighter in this dark world. This doesn't mean He loves them more, for the security and love established in Christ is unchangeable. But it does mean we reflect Him more accurately and beautifully to the world around us when we are **self-controlled**, for He is. Elders were held to this standard in their character and as a part of the mandate to be **above reproach.**

We've explored how elders are above reproach in their families and their character, now we arrive at the third and final category of our list—items that reveal an elder's commitment to ministry within the church. A vital part of an elder's ministry was **holding fast the faithful word which is in accordance with the teaching.**

What a beautiful image **holding fast** brings to our mind. We imagine the rigid grip of a mountaineer on the edge of a mountain as he makes his treacherous climb. Or the white knuckles of a sailor grabbing ropes to control the sails of a ship being tossed on enormous waves. Although these are physical examples, they evoke the emotion and spiritual intensity needed to accomplish what Paul mandates here. Elders were to grip the **faithful word** (i.e., the gospel and all the doctrine therein) with such intensity, it was as if their life and breath depended on it.

The **faithful word** they grasped was **in accordance with the teaching** that Paul and the other apostles had communicated. These teachings were based on Christ, His ministry, His mission, His fulfillment of Old Testament prophecy, and His instigation of a new era of salvation. The apostles also had a special anointing from the Holy Spirit, who revealed truth and doctrine to them as they went. Remember, they didn't have the completed New Testament, they were living it out and writing it as they learned.[68]

Not having completed Scripture made this faithful adherence to the teaching of the gospel tricky. Numerous people arose over the years (we will see examples forthwith) and took advantage of the situation, warping the gospel for their own benefit. Fortunately, Paul, Titus, and other apostles and apostolic delegates were thoroughly trained, committed, and loyal to the truth. They also had a built-in network of accountability with each other to prevent anyone from straying in his theology. Elders had to follow in the apostles' footsteps and remain dedicated to the **faithful word which is in accordance with the teaching** they had received and believed.

Holding fast to the faithful word was crucial to the elder's primary purpose of ministry—**so that he will be able to both exhort in sound doctrine and refute those who contradict.** This mandate was the crown to all the elders' responsibilities, for it is what the fledgling church needed most. Paul already wrote about **the knowledge of the truth** as one of his central tenants to apostleship, and he knew how imperative it is for elders to adopt such a tenant as their own. The term **exhort** (*parakaleo*) is rich with the idea of encouragement and beseeching. The gospel is not a set of facts to be taught as much as hope to be compelled to. In teaching sound doctrine, elders also encouraged and imparted their own passion for the gospel with the intent of drawing others to God, just as they were.

Sound doctrine both elicits exhortation and demands preservation, calling elders to **refute those who contradict** it. Because Satan will always try to thwart any and every advancement of the gospel, those in church leadership must be prepared. Preparation comes first by knowing the truth intimately, for the deeper we are rooted in truth, the harder it will be for lies to blow us over. Yet knowledge accomplishes nothing without partnering with action—operational belief and weeding out any falsities that try to creep into our hearts and minds. The elders were both truth advancers and preservers, called to exhort and protect the gospel as their primary function in ministry.

Unfortunately, their task was not easy, because they had active enemies pushing against the gospel.

FOR THERE ARE MANY REBELLIOUS MEN, EMPTY TALKERS AND DECEIVERS, ESPECIALLY THOSE OF THE CIRCUMCISION, WHO MUST BE SILENCED BECAUSE THEY ARE UPSETTING WHOLE FAMILIES, TEACHING THINGS THEY SHOULD NOT TEACH FOR THE SAKE OF SORDID GAIN.

Elders did not simply teach the ancient equivalent of Sunday School and spend the rest of their time socializing and saying kind words to church members. They were warriors fighting in a fierce and sometimes dangerous war for the souls around them. Adversaries were real, hostile. They actively combated gospel efforts through open rebellion, misleading words, and fraudulent teaching.

These **rebellious men** were **especially those of the circumcision**, which means they were Jews who, although professing to know Christ, hindered the gospel from gaining ground. Their incomplete and erroneous theology was no doubt fueled by lingering Jewish arrogance (since Judaism had, until this point, been the sole conduit of genuine faith in God). The corrupt Cretan society they lived in surely didn't help either. Wanting to be in control and profit from a gross misunderstanding of the gospel, they armed themselves with verbal weapons in an effort to strike down any truth that made it into church members' hearts.

The childhood rhyme, "Sticks and stones may break my bones, but words will never hurt me" is a myth. Words are dangerous, perhaps even more so than physical harm, because they inflict damage to our souls, not just to flesh that heals. **Empty talkers and deceivers** are those who confuse and distract others with nonsense and worthless topics. Such irrelevant talk, disguised as important by these deceivers, prevents others from absorbing the truth of the gospel.

Because of their ill intentions and damaging words, Paul announces they **must be silenced**. No, Paul does not form an underground mob with this statement, planning to eliminate any and all competition permanently.

Rather, he's instructing Titus to silence them by reason. "The way to combat false teaching is to offer true teaching," and the only true teaching incapable of falling is that of the gospel.[69] If the enemy is loud, be louder with the truth. Titus and the elders he was recruiting needed to be louder with the truth than their theological enemies were with their worthless verbal vomit.

Titus couldn't allow the rebellious men to continue in their deception, because they were **upsetting whole families.** While this can and did include individual family units, the greater focus here is most likely on individual church families.[70] Since congregations met in homes, they experienced community in a deeper, more intimate way than most Americans experience in their church gathering places. It's not difficult to imagine, then, the influence of a rebellious man on such a modest crowd. The church was still relatively new to Crete, and congregants were hungry for knowledge. It would've been easy for them to be led astray by men placing themselves in positions of authority.

Even worse than **upsetting whole families** is the fact that they were **teaching things they should not teach for the sake of sordid gain.** We're not told how they profited from their erroneous teaching, but we'd be remiss to ignore this repeat of the phrase **sordid gain.** In the character category of our elder qualification list, we read that elders must be men **not fond of sordid gain.** Thus, these rebellious Jewish men were the exact opposite of what a true elder—a true leader—should be. Not only did they cause distress among churches by worthless teaching, they profited from it. They embodied everything a true elder wasn't—selfish, self-willed, deceitful, loving what is wrong, and making a profit off their depraved and false leadership.

ONE OF THEMSELVES, A PROPHET OF THEIR OWN, SAID, "CRETANS ARE ALWAYS LIARS, EVIL BEASTS, LAZY GLUTTONS."

To fortify his point, Paul quotes Epimenides, a notorious ancient philosopher and acclaimed prophet,[71] saying **one of themselves, a prophet of their own, said, "Cretans are always liars, evil beasts, lazy gluttons."** Epimenides was not a prophet in the biblical sense, for prophets of God were specifically appointed by Him to communicate with His people. Every prophecy they spoke had to materialize (because God cannot lie), otherwise they would be put to death.[72] Rather, Epimenides, **a prophet of their own**, could be considered on the same plane as Aristotle or Plato, someone revered and held in high esteem for his wisdom and philosophical meanderings.

As we've mentioned, Cretans possessed a shocking lack of morals. They believed highway robbery was honorable and that personal gain was admirable, regardless of how it was accumulated.[73] Cretans exuded a particular stench of sin detected only in the deepest bowels of human depravity. The accusations of being **always liars, evil beasts, lazy gluttons** were rather mild, then, considering.

The astute will recognize a perplexing irony in Paul's statement, though. If a Cretan says that **"Cretans are always liars, evil beasts, lazy gluttons,"** then is he lying in saying that? One scholar dissects the dichotomy as follows:

> If Cretans are always liars, and if the speaker … is a Cretan, then he must be a liar. And if he is a liar, then his "testimony" cannot be true. On the other hand, if it is true that Cretans are always liars, then his testimony corresponds to the facts of the case and he is not lying. But this would mean that not all Cretans are lying all the time, which would mean that the beginning premise was false. So if he is lying, then he is telling the truth (when he says that Cretans are always liars); and if he is telling the truth, then he must be lying (since he himself disproves the stated rule that Cretans are always liars).[74]

Confused yet? It's supposed to be. The nonsensical hypocrisy of Paul's quote is meant to be ridiculous. Why? To point out the nonsensical hypocrisy the **empty talkers and deceivers** are spewing forth to the Cretan church.[75] They expel murky gloom; true elders proclaim unambiguous light. The gospel's light shocked the curdled darkness that had settled upon the Cretans' hearts, and it was the leaders' job to fuel the flame.

THIS TESTIMONY IS TRUE. FOR THIS REASON REPROVE THEM SEVERELY SO THAT THEY MAY BE SOUND IN THE FAITH, NOT PAYING ATTENTION TO JEWISH MYTHS AND COMMANDMENTS OF MEN WHO TURN AWAY FROM THE TRUTH.

Because **this testimony is true,** Paul urged Titus to take action, reproving these men and ignoring their deceiving ways.

Leadership requires a lot of work, especially when dealing with the muddled issues of the early Cretan church. We've seen expectations for elders in ministry; now Paul turns his attention directly to Titus once again. He implores Titus to **reprove them**—Cretan false teachers, Jewish and Gentile alike. The word **reprove** here is the same as **refute** in verse 9, describing an elder's responsibility to **refute those who contradict** sound doctrine. Titus receives an added sense of urgency in this particular instruction, though, with the addition of **severely.** Certain situations demand a heavier hand of correction than others, and if ever an egregious society needed stern intervention, it was Crete.

Titus' reprimand possesses a greater purpose than mere chastisement. The objective was **that they may be sound in the faith.** Any disciplinary action within ministry should have the ultimate goal of transformation, restoration, and reconciliation. By weeding out and silencing **Jewish myths and commandments of men who turn away from the truth**, Titus would help people understand the gospel. When **sound doctrine** is restored and realized, ministry flourishes, as do the souls of people within the church.

Despite the foolhardiness of the Cretans, Paul doesn't tell Titus to cast them off, reject them, or leave them in their hopeless state. Rather, he's saying, "They are bad and we all know it. *Go and convert them.*"[76] How amazing this is! I love Barclay's summary of this thought:

> Few passages so demonstrate the divine optimism of the Christian evangelist who refuses to regard anyone as hopeless. The greater the evil, the greater the challenge. It is the Christian conviction that there is no sin too great for the grace of Jesus Christ to conquer.[77]

As long as we breathe, we hope and have hope. Not even truth-distorting, deceiving rebels could stop God from reaching the hearts of the Cretan church.

Paul concludes this section of his letter with a commentary regarding the rebels:

TO THE PURE, ALL THINGS ARE PURE; BUT TO THOSE WHO ARE DEFILED AND UNBELIEVING, NOTHING IS PURE, BUT BOTH THEIR MINDS AND THEIR CONSCIENCE ARE DEFILED. THEY PROFESS TO KNOW GOD, BUT BY THEIR DEEDS THEY DENY HIM, BEING DETESTABLE AND DISOBEDIENT AND WORTHLESS FOR ANY GOOD DEED.

The Jewish nature of the rebels immediately catches our eye in these verses, drawing our minds back to Jesus' many confrontations with Jewish leaders. Jewish leaders, particularly the Pharisees, prided themselves on the religious and holy image they created for themselves. To boost their pious persona, they adhered to ridiculous self-imposed rules and regulations, ironically neglecting God and what He truly desired—their love and worship.[78]

This puff of pride—the convolution of sound doctrine by adding worthless nonsense to it—captures Paul's condemnation. But he begins with a positive note, **to the pure, all things are pure.** The clear example here is the issue of food, which was still a sticking point for Jews who called themselves Christians. Under the Old Testament law, Jews were prohibited from eating certain "unclean" foods: pork, rabbits, certain kinds of fish, birds like eagles, vultures, and ravens, etc.[79] When Christ came, He fulfilled the law and set us free from it, making anything permissible for consumption. "It is not what enters into the mouth that defiles the man, but what proceeds out of the mouth, this defiles the man."[80] Thus, those in Christ are pure and can partake of any kind of food (and a host of other once-considered-unclean activities) and still be pure. We are free from the restraints of the law.

But because habits are hard to break (particularly habits cemented into law that governed a people group for centuries), the Jews were still having a difficult time letting certain ones go. Their minds were **defiled and unbelieving**—defiled by the law that no longer governed them, and unbelieving the freedom they had in Christ. **Nothing is pure** to those burdened by self-imposed and unnecessary rules and regulations. Everything is tainted because **both their minds and their conscience are defiled** by their erroneous beliefs.

Think of eyeglasses. They help people with vision impairments to see better, if not perfectly. Now imagine smearing mud all over the lenses of your glasses before putting them on. Not very helpful, right? That's what false teachings did for the rebellious Jewish men advocating them—they mucked up their vision of everything in their lives. The problem is that the rebels got so used to them, they preferred that view to the spotless lenses Christ offers through the gospel.

Such men **profess to know God,** and while they may certainly know *of* Him, they are not in a personal, thriving relationship *with* Him through

Jesus Christ. They talk *about* Him but not *to* Him; they stand *before* Him but are not secured *in* Him.

While we can never know the hearts of people around us, their lives give us clues. The qualifications of elders were exactly that—parameters by which lives could be measured to see if they were equipped to lead people within the church. The faulty Jewish men were also measured by their actions, but instead of glorifying Christ—**by their deeds they deny Him, being detestable and disobedient and worthless for any good deed.**

Their teachings were as worthless as their actions. They had no problem obeying human commands (especially ones originating with them), but were disobedient to God's (the only ones that matter).[81]

The contrast between true elders and false teachers in this passage is stark, which is Paul's intention. Leaders carry great influence, either drawing people closer to God or pulling them away. The direction of a leader's agenda, while not foolproof, can be deduced by their actions and the way they live. If they adhere to the elder qualifications listed by Paul in this passage, they will be worthy to lead Christians within a church context and, more importantly, closer to God's heart. If, on the other hand, they possess markers of the Jewish rebellious men, it's clear their agenda is to serve their own selfish purposes, not advance the gospel. Titus was given the task to discover both kinds of leader—investing time, energy, and prayer in those who would become elders, and severely refuting those spewing erroneous teaching so they may be restored.

GROUP STUDY

INTRODUCTION

The power of leadership comes not from position, but from influence.

Leaders permeate every aspect of our culture and communities. From individual homes to the highest forms of governments and world powers, leaders rise up and impact the people around them. Good leaders make us want to follow and even emulate them, accomplishing great things in this world. Bad leaders make us cringe and want to get out from under their authority, as they wreak havoc on everyone within their circles of influence.

- Tell us about someone in your life who is (or has been) a great leader.
- Have you been under the authority of an awful leader? How did that experience impact you?

THE WORD

Titus was given the task of identifying two kinds of leaders within the Cretan church—admirable men who lived above reproach and were qualified to be elders, and rebellious men who were leading congregants astray with their lies and worthless teaching. Paul provided Titus with a list of cues to look for in identifying both:

> Among other things, an elder must be "above reproach as God's steward … holding fast the faithful word which is in accordance with the teaching, so that he will be able both to exhort in sound doctrine and to refute those who contradict." (Titus 1:7a, 9)

Rebellious men, on the other hand, were "empty talkers and deceivers, especially those of the circumcision … They profess to know God, but by their deeds they deny Him, being detestable and disobedient and worthless for any good deed." Because of this, they were to be "silenced" and reproved "severely so that they may be sound in the faith." (Titus 1:10, 11, 16, 13b)

- In what ways is being "above reproach" a high standard?

- What must the elder hold fast to in his life and ministry?

  - Why must he hold fast to it?

- In what two ways were rebellious men identified?

  _____ talkers and _____

  - Why do you think those were particularly dangerous traits for a new church?

- What was the relationship between their words and deeds?

  - How do words and deeds typically reveal the status of our faith?

- What action was Titus supposed to take against them?

  - How is this response one of hope?

APPLY

While we may never hold positions of great leadership within the church (or elsewhere), we must acknowledge that we all hold positions of *influence* on people around us. Our words, actions, and choices matter because people are watching.

> Be imitators of me, just as I also am of Christ.
> The Apostle Paul, 1 Corinthians 11:1

> For I gave you an example that you also should do as I did to you.
> Jesus, John 13:15

As Christians, our goal in leadership is to be transformed into the image of Christ and help others do the same. Just as elders did in the early church, we are to live "above reproach" so people crave Jesus simply by being in our presence and lives.

- How is your life, generally speaking, "above reproach" right now?

  - In what areas are you growing spiritually?

  - What area is currently a work in progress?

- Who are three individuals you have influence over?

  - _____

  - _____

  - _____

- Take some time to evaluate your influence on them this week:

  - Are your responses revealing Christ to them?

  - Is your attitude one of encouragement or criticism?

  - If you were the only Christian they knew, what would Christ look like to them, based on your life?

  - Every day this week, ask (or beg!) God to transform your life so you can inspire others to do likewise.

WEEK THREE
TITUS 2:1-10

PERSONAL BIBLE STUDY QUESTIONS

1. What was Titus supposed to speak? (2:1)

2. What character traits are becoming for older men? (2:2)

   a)

   b)

   c)

   d)

   e)

   f)

3. Who in your life demonstrates these traits? What impact have these people had on your life?

4. What character traits should present themselves in older women? (2:3-4)

   a)

   b)

   c)

   d)

   e)

5. Has anyone like this mentored you? How did you (or would you)
   benefit from being mentored by such a person?

6. Young women should be encouraged to ... (2:4-5)

7.

   a)

   b)

   c)

   d)

   e)

   f)

   g)

8. How do you think society would be different if young women
   were known by these traits?

9. Young men were to be _____. (2:6)

10. Titus was instructed to... (2:7-8)

    a)

    b)

    c)

    d)

11. Bondslaves were to be... (2:9-10)

    a)

    b)

    c)

    d)

    e)

COMMENTARY

But as for you, speak the things which are fitting for sound doctrine. Older men are to be temperate, dignified, sensible, sound in faith, in love, in perseverance. Older women likewise are to be reverent in their behavior, not malicious gossips nor enslaved to much wine, teaching what is good, so that they may encourage the young women to love their husbands, to love their children, to be sensible, pure, workers at home, kind, being subject to their own husbands, so that the word of God will not be dishonored. Likewise urge the young men to be sensible; in all things show yourself to be an example of good deeds, with purity in doctrine, dignified, sound in speech which is beyond reproach, so that the opponent will be put to shame, having nothing bad to say about us. Urge bondslaves to be subject to their own masters in everything, to be well-pleasing, not argumentative, not pilfering, but showing all good faith so that they will adorn the doctrine of God our Savior in every respect.

Titus 2:1-10

One distinctly Christian aspect of life is beauty. Other religions and worldviews may acknowledge that beauty exists, but it doesn't serve a purpose or bear any spiritual meaning beyond that. Christianity, however, secures an origin of beauty (God), and a purpose for it (to be celebrated and enjoyed by all of creation).[82] Even amidst a theologically dark and decaying world, beauty surrounds us—in a new tiny sprout that emerges through recently scorched earth, in the laughter of an infant giggling for the first time, in the vastness of the wilderness when observed from a mountain peak. We see it in the vibrant colors of sea creatures that dwell deep in ocean waters, in the fathomless mural of celestial beings that make up the sky, or in the eyes of a groom as he beholds his bride walking down the aisle. Beauty manifests itself in endless ways. It's a gift given to us by God Himself.

Paul points us to an intriguing manifestation of beauty in this passage, particularly in relationship to the gospel. We (as Christians) can make the gospel beautiful by the way we live. Our actions not only reflect our relationship with Christ and influence others for Him, but they also can make His truth beautiful in the eyes of the world. The gospel, beautiful on its own, becomes irresistible when exercised in the lives of those who believe.

While this is all great in theory, Paul doesn't want it to remain in the land of philosophical ponderings. So he gives Titus another list. It contains directions for what this looks like in real life, which would've been especially important amidst the putrid Cretan culture. How is the gospel made beautiful in the lives of Christians? Let's find out.

BUT AS FOR YOU, SPEAK THE THINGS WHICH ARE FITTING FOR SOUND DOCTRINE.

As with any letter or personal correspondence today, the book of Titus was not originally broken down into chapters and verses. Paul didn't pause at his thoughts to make sure each one was appropriately marked with chapter and verse numbers (though that's obvious, considering his penchant for run-on sentences!). Rather, it flowed from his mind via the inspiration of God through ink onto the parchment paper laid out before him.

When we arrive at a conjunction word (typically found at the beginning of verses and chapters), it's imperative that we pause to note the thoughts it connects. Here Paul connects (and in this case, contrasts) his commentary on the rebellious men from the end of chapter one with Titus, his protégé. Rebellious men **profess to know God, but by their deeds they deny Him, being detestable and disobedient and worthless for any good deed. <u>But as for you,</u>** (Titus) **speak the things which are fitting for sound doctrine** (emphasis added). Titus stands distinct from the chastised rebellious men of chapter one. Instead of spewing out lies and other worthless discourses that distract from the gospel, Titus was commissioned to **speak things which are fitting for sound doctrine.**

Words are powerful in their own merit. When they contain the gospel message, their power is ignited to limitless capacities, because their ultimate origin is the Infinite. Titus and other apostles harnessed this power and unleashed it through their teachings, rebuttals of false doctrine, and encouragement to their congregants. They actively fought against the deception that crept into the Cretan church. They also inspired others to grow in the knowledge of the truth (as Paul's apostleship mission said in chapter one).

Sound doctrine, again, refers to the gospel and the myriad of ways it impacts our daily lives. While the gospel is specifically the good news of Jesus Christ and the salvation He brings to the world, on a broader scale it encompasses everything that news implies—our justification, sanctification, adoption into His family, our purpose in this life, our relationships, hope, our behavior, etc. The Cretans needed help in two specific areas: first, they needed help understanding the gospel from an intellectual standpoint. It was so new to them, they needed to learn its core, facts, and nuances so it would fuse to their minds. Faith requires knowledge, and knowledge precipitates any further growth in faith. Because of the surrounding culture, the second thing the Cretans needed help with was their lifestyle/behavior. They needed to learn how to make the gospel beautiful to the world around them via their actions and lives.

By speaking the gospel and its implications for life, Titus obeyed Paul by speaking **the things which are fitting for sound doctrine.** But Paul doesn't leave Titus to sort through all those implications and then decide what to teach on his own. Rather, he provides him with another list, this one containing attributes for specific gender, age, and social status combinations.

OLDER MEN ARE TO BE TEMPERATE, DIGNIFIED, SENSIBLE, SOUND IN
FAITH, IN LOVE, IN PERSEVERANCE.

Older men are the first gender and age group Paul addresses. In biblical times, **older men** were "at least somewhere upward of forty years old, possibly into their fifties or sixties,"[83] men whose ages were "sufficient to have raised a family and seen their children begin families of their own."[84] This term is rare, used only two other times in the New Testament. While **older men** were "natural leaders of the community,"[85] Paul is not speaking specifically of the elders from our first list in chapter one (though elders were certainly held to any and all standards laid out for the congregation). Rather, these are **older men** in general—any man considered of age within the community of believers.

These **older men** were first required **to be temperate**. This term (*nephalios*) is also rare, and like **older men**, occurs only two other times in the New Testament. Also translated as "sober," this term, when used symbolically as our context demands, connotes the idea of being "free from every form of excess, passion, or rashness."[86] Pursuing self-pleasure via wine or any other inappropriate indulgence marks youthful foolishness, not seasoned wisdom. **Older men** should've learned long ago that "the pleasures of self-indulgence cost far more than they are worth,"[87] and adopted a mentality of being **temperate** as a result.

Along with temperance, **older men** were to be **dignified** members of their community and church. We have yet another rare word (*senmos*), used only four times throughout the New Testament. It's used elsewhere in a beloved passage:

> Finally, brethren, whatever is true, whatever is honorable (*senmos*), whatever is right, whatever is pure, whatever is lovely, whatever is of good repute, if there is any excellence and if anything worthy of praise, dwell on these things.[88]

Dignified men were reverent, worthy of respect, and serious. Despite such weighty definitions, this term does not translate as men being gloomy grouches who sucked the life and fun out of everyone around them. Rather, these men lived with an acute awareness of eternity in all aspects of their earthly lives.[89] They saw through the temporally urgent and irrelevant to the eternal, translating the physical through spiritual eyes. Such spiritual maturity undoubtedly made them distinct in their surrounding pagan culture.

Distinction in dignity carried into distinction in sensibleness. **Older men** were to be **sensible** in their age and positions within their families and community. This term is translated in other Bible versions as temperate, to live wisely, self-controlled, and sober-minded. Synonyms range, but the idea is that **older men** should show "a measured restraint in all things— the opposite of the behavior that might be regarded as foolish or 'Cretan.'"[90] Cretans indulged in whatever whims caught their attention and base desires; Christians (particularly older, wiser men among them) were to evaluate situations and opportunities from a spiritual perspective, making **sensible** choices that reflected the God they served.

The last expectation of **older men** was to be **sound** in three ways—**in faith, in love, and in perseverance.** This word is used often in this book (1:9, 1:13, 2:1), referring to doctrine as well as one's character. To be **sound** is to be established, mature, resolute, or strong. **Older men** were to be sound "in every aspect of their character," so it described their personhood more than one particular aspect.[91]

Paul has three particular components in mind that encompass one's whole soundness: **in faith, in love, and in perseverance.** Scripture defines faith as "the assurance of things hoped for, the conviction of things not seen."[92] Faith is confidence that God is who He says He is, and has done/will do what He says. Soundness **in faith,** then, "depicts the invisible dimension of Christian existence, focusing on the activity of believing (in the gospel, in God/Christ) that determines Christian identity and expresses the human response to God."[93] It's impossible to please God without faith, so being sound in faith seems an apt requirement for men heavily influencing their homes, churches, and communities.[94]

The heartbeat of Christianity is **love.** God is love, the gospel is the ultimate expression of love, and those who accept it are (or should be) marked by love. "The one who does not love does not know God, for God is love."[95] **Older men,** then, absolutely must be **sound ... in love.** Love serves as a great example of the marriage between knowledge and behavior required for Christians (including Cretan believers). In order to love well, one must first understand God's love for us. God chose to love us despite our blatant and perpetual rejection of Him, culminated His expression of love by sending His Son to die so we might live, and continues to love by drawing people close to His heart. To be **sound in love,** we must intellectually comprehend and affirm these basic facts.

But intellectual assertion is not enough. To be truly **sound in love,** we must embrace knowledge in our lives and behavior. Knowing *that* and *how* God loves us motivates us to love others:

> Beloved, let us love one another, for love is from God; and everyone who loves is born of God and knows God. The one who does not love does not know God, for God is love. By this the love of God was manifested in us, that God has sent His only begotten Son into the world so that we might live through Him. In this is love, not that we have loved God, but that He loved us and sent His Son to be the propitiation for our sins. Beloved, if God so loved us, we also ought to love one another. No one has seen God at any time; if we love one another, God abides in us, and His love is perfected in us.[96]

Older men must be **sound in love** in order to be genuine and acceptable representatives of Christ. Ill behavior toward others does not reflect Christ in any way, shape, or form, and thus should not be present in the lives of those who call Him Lord.

Concluding the elements of soundness in an older man's life is that of **perseverance.** This is a common term throughout the New Testament and is also translated as patience, endurance, and steadfastness. In light of the particularly hideous state of Cretan society, **perseverance** would've been a desperately needed quality for any Christian. Even more so, Christian **older men** were expected to have shown and been examples of it. To persevere means to make wise and eternally significant decisions consistently, regardless of trial or circumstance.

We can think of perseverance as building habits. Habits are formed when we make consistent decisions every day for about a month. The same can be said for spiritual disciplines. When we are consistent in our choices, from reading the Bible every day to being honest regardless of the consequences, we persevere in the application of our faith. The more we do this, the greater our chances of remaining faithful, even when times are tough. Perseverance doesn't make us perfect, but it does make the gospel that much more beautiful in our lives.

Older men are commissioned to live in a way that attracts others to the gospel. They're to be **temperate, dignified, sensible, sound in faith, in love, in perseverance.** Even if they didn't hold an official position within the church, older men heavily influenced the world around them. Bringing these character traits to life adorned the sound doctrine they had embraced both intellectually and behaviorally.

OLDER WOMEN LIKEWISE ARE TO BE REVERENT IN THEIR BEHAVIOR, NOT MALICIOUS GOSSIPS NOR ENSLAVED TO MUCH WINE, TEACHING WHAT IS GOOD ...

We now arrive at one of the most popular passages among women's ministries all over the country. The "Titus 2 Woman" has inspired several books and articles, countless talks, and even conference themes. While there are undoubtedly several fabulous truths to uncover from this passage, our goal is to discover the truths while keeping them within their immediate context. Individual passages can absolutely undergo proper exegesis for thorough application. But many are studied as silos—removed from their immediate contexts and interpreted as singular thoughts. While it may be possible to receive correct applications this way, this method is inherently dangerous. Removing any part of Scripture from its direct context and then from the overarching context of the gospel makes interpretations and applications ripe for heresy.

Our context is the book of Titus, a letter written by the apostle Paul to Titus, one of his dear protégés. He writes to encourage and instruct Titus, who remained behind in Crete to establish the young church there. This encouragement and instruction has thus far included an introduction of Paul and his mission as an apostle, a helpful list of qualities that should be present in every elder candidate, a warning about false teachers deceiving members of the church, a reminder for Titus to speak the truth, and now gender/age group characteristics that glorify the gospel in the lives of those who believe.

Older women are a specific gender and age group Paul targets with his instruction for holy living. These women, **likewise** to their male counterparts, are to reflect and advance Christ and His gospel. Doing so requires them first **to be reverent in their behavior.** This phrase can also be translated as to live in a way that honors God or to exhibit behavior fitting for those who are holy.[97] The term **reverent** (*hieroprepes*) is used only here in the Greek text, and is often translated simply as holy in other ancient texts.[98] Holiness means to be set apart, consecrated for God. Holy behavior, therefore, would mean that these women were to be distinct from the corrupt society around them.

Another more specialized definition exists for *hieroprepes*, however. It can also mean to act like a priestess, "resulting from its use to describe the conduct of a priest."[99] While the broader definition certainly reflects the context, this one does too, with a unique twist. Christ served as our ultimate High Priest, so the priesthood as Jews knew it was finished. But the imagery was still alive in their minds as they processed Christ's role in the new (and final) era of their faith.

> ... Jesus has become the guarantee of a better covenant. The former priests, on the one hand, existed in greater numbers because they were prevented by death from continuing, but Jesus, on the other hand, because He continues forever, holds His priesthood permanently. Therefore He is able also to save forever those who draw near to God through Him, since He always lives to make intercession for them. For it was fitting for us to have such a high priest, *holy, innocent, undefiled, separated from sinners* and exalted above the heavens; who does not need daily, like those high priests, to offer up sacrifices, first for His own sins and then for the sins of the people, because this He did once for all when He offered up Himself. For the Law appoints men as high priests who are weak, but the word of the oath, which came after the Law, appoints a Son, made perfect forever.[100]

Priesthood was a very big deal in Judaism, for it foreshadowed the coming Messiah, who would be (and was in Christ) the final priest. Believers in Christ are also referred to as a priesthood:

> You also, as living stones, are being built up as a spiritual house for a holy priesthood, to offer up spiritual sacrifices acceptable to God through Jesus Christ ... you are a chosen race, a royal priesthood, a holy nation, a people for God's own possession, so that you may proclaim the excellencies of Him who has called you out of darkness into His marvelous light.[101]

Christians are at their core "little Christs" following their namesake and becoming like Him in the mission of advancing the gospel on earth.

Priesthood is one metaphor to describe the agents of this mission—specifically commissioned by God to be His and proclaim His truth to a dark world. **Reverent** (or holy) **behavior**, then, could absolutely carry with it the idea of **older women** conducting themselves as priestesses—both from a former Jewish mindset suggesting the seriousness and weight of such a title, and from the new era of faith Christ ushered into the world, making all believers a part of His royal priesthood.

Women **reverent in their behavior** are also women who are **not malicious gossips.** Stereotypes exist for a reason—women love to talk! Sometimes even the most well-intentioned talk (even under the guise of prayer requests) becomes gossip that can destroy trust, community, and reputations. **Older women** especially needed to beware of this temptation, since they were more likely to have extra time in their day. Tasks and chores decreased with age due to children growing and leaving their homes, and perhaps even the physical ability to perform duties diminished as joints aged and bodies slowed down. A major temptation with extra time, then, would be to catch up on (or ignite) community gossip.

Gossip is speaking negatively of someone, regardless of the truthfulness of the information. In Proverbs, God warns that "he who goes about as a slanderer reveals secrets, therefore do not associate with a gossip."[102] Did you catch that? We aren't even to associate with someone who is known to gossip. This may seem harsh, but not when we dig a little deeper and switch to Greek word origins. "The word "devil" "comes from the Greek root *diabolos*, meaning "slanderer." Those persons who cannot control their tongues, speaking lies and false accusations and spreading malicious gossip (whether true or untrue) do the work of Satan himself."[103] Yikes. Gossip is a manifestation of Satan's very name, not to mention the venomous work he commits himself to.

Being **reverent in their behavior** leaves no room for gossip; the same for being **enslaved to much wine.** This trait sounds familiar, as it is basically the repeat of an elder qualification in chapter one of this letter, calling for elders not to be **addicted to wine.** Again, alcohol is neither good nor bad, moral nor immoral. It is merely an object we can use for either enjoyment or inappropriate purposes. This is true for many things people become addicted to—prescription drugs, gambling, food, coffee, anger, the internet, smoking, work, shopping, etc. While some of these should probably be avoided altogether (smoking, gambling, etc.), others are legitimate parts of life that people sometimes allow to take control of their lives.

Both gossip and alcohol addiction stem from a root issue of a lack of self-control. Or more accurately, a lack of being controlled by the Holy Spirit. If we "walk by the Spirit," we will "not carry out the desire of the flesh."[104] **Older women** in the church were to allow the Spirit to control them so they wouldn't carry out fleshly desires like gossip or alcohol.

In addition to avoiding gossip and alcohol, **older women** were to be active in **teaching what is good.** This is not the same kind of teaching that the apostles or elders carried out.[105] The differences between apostolic teaching and women's teaching were twofold: in method and in subject. Women did not teach formally like apostles or elders, meaning they did not deliver sermons or perform Scriptural exegesis to gathered coed members of a church. This does not mean they were incapable of doing so, or were somehow unable to receive the spiritual gift of teaching. Rather, their appropriate, God-designed modes of teaching leaned more toward helping other women understand and apply the gospel to their daily lives and conduct.

Just as men are the only gender permitted to serve in the position of elder, so are men the only gender approved for formal theological teaching in a mix-gendered congregational assembly of the church. The difficulty of this subject is immense, just as the questions and emotions that arise when studying it. And just like our previous discussion, any examination of the subject here will undoubtedly leave questions unanswered and emotions unresolved. But we aren't at liberty to ignore or gloss over parts of the Bible that aren't comfortable, so we will make a few observations and leave further study to experts who have more thoroughly tackled the subject.[106]

As discussed previously, God created men and women equal in value, yet different in design and function. We execute different roles in relationships and within church leadership. In relationships, wives are given clear instruction:

> Wives, be subject to your own husbands, as to the Lord. For the husband is the head of the wife, as Christ also is the head of the church, He Himself being the Savior of the body. But as the church is subject to Christ, so also the wives ought to be to their husbands in everything.[107]

Two notes on this. First, being *subject* does not mean being *slaves*. Women were not and are not voiceless beings expected to carry out every desire and whim of their husbands. Some men have preached this despicable and heretical translation over the years. They should be silenced just as Titus was to silence the Jewish deceivers in chapter one. In reality, being subject means to willingly support, encourage, follow, and yield to one's husband as God's appointed leader of the household.

Before getting too worked up, let's look at the expectations placed on husbands:

> Husbands, love your wives, just as Christ also loved the church and gave Himself up for her, so that He might sanctify her, having cleansed her by the washing of water with the word, that He might present to Himself the church in all her glory, having no spot or wrinkle or any such thing; but that she would be holy and blameless. So husbands ought also to love their own wives as their own bodies. He who loves his own wife loves himself; for

no one ever hated his own flesh, but nourishes and cherishes it, just as Christ also does the church, because we are members of His body. For this reason a man shall leave his father and mother and shall be joined to his wife, and the two shall become one flesh. This mystery is great; but I am speaking with reference to Christ and the church. Nevertheless, each individual among you also is to love his own wife even as himself, and the wife must see to it that she respects her husband.[108]

Women are to yield lovingly to their husbands; husbands are to sacrifice everything—their very own lives, dreams, and desires, if necessary—to love their wives. Husbands actively submit to Christ as they sacrificially love their wives and do everything within their power to draw their marriage closer to God. In other words, men bear a far greater burden in marriage (and in general relationships between men and women). The connection plunges deeper in meaning as Paul (in Ephesians) compares marriage roles to those of Christ and the church. The church has responsibilities, to be sure—to love and follow Christ. But Christ accomplished way more for the church than the church will ever do in return. Thus, it's not demeaning for women (or the church) to be told to follow their husbands and yield to them. Rather, it's an honor and relief to follow someone who's given up everything for them—whose mission in life is to love them with a fierceness and loyalty known only by Christ Himself.

We must have this perspective in mind when interpreting our passage in Titus. Women were not permitted to teach formal doctrine, in a formal manner, to men. Now, knowing the posture that men and women were (and are) to have with each other, this doesn't seem like a restriction as much as much as an opportunity to help gender roles flourish as God designed them. By teaching only other women, women allow men to fulfill their intense and weighty roles as sacrificial leaders as they subsequently submit to Christ.

Since we live in a broken world and the church is made up of sinful people, neither gender fulfills these roles perfectly as God ordained them. But our obedience is not dependent on our peers' obedience. We obey in a response of utmost gratitude for Christ and what He's done for us. When we do, we experience emotional and spiritual benefits—personally as well as in our marriages, families, churches, and communities.

Knowledge is the first step to life transformation (with gender roles as well as with any truth). The next step is practice. If we commit ourselves to learning and applying God's Word, we align ourselves with Him, grow astronomically in our relationships with Him and others, and make His truth that much more attractive to the world around us, drawing others to the gospel.

SO THAT THEY MAY ENCOURAGE THE YOUNG WOMEN TO LOVE THEIR HUSBANDS, TO LOVE THEIR CHILDREN, TO BE SENSIBLE, PURE, WORKERS AT HOME, KIND, BEING SUBJECT TO THEIR OWN HUSBANDS, SO THAT THE WORD OF GOD WILL NOT BE DISHONORED.

The kind of teaching **older women** were called to do primarily regarded pouring encouragement and truth into **young women** as they navigated their lives with this newfound faith in Christ. This calling was especially important, considering the baseness of the Cretan society they once embraced. It's also interesting to note that training the younger women was not a direct responsibility of Titus.[109] Just as Paul empowered Titus' leadership, so Titus is empowering older women's leadership to blossom and take its full effect in the lives of the women under their authority within the church. And frankly, young women probably appreciated such authentic and personal instruction from other women, who understood their daily lives and struggles far better than men would.

Encourage here is tough to translate for several reasons, but "in the present context … understanding the verb (and therefore the nature of the teaching to be given) as a jolting 'call to return to the senses' seems most suitable."[110] In other words, **older women** were to teach **what is good so that they may encourage** (or vigorously remind) **the young women to** continue becoming women who beautify the gospel with their lifestyle and behaviors.

First on the list for younger women is the admonition **to love their husbands.** This wasn't just an action required by God; it was also praised by both Hellenistic and Jewish cultures—"the presence of this kind of love indicated an exceptional wife."[111] The concept of marital love was different in New Testament times than it is today. Parents arranged marriages for the mutual benefit of both families, though many did consider compatibility when making their decisions. Love wasn't a major factor when joining a man and wife together in matrimony, because marriages were of convenience and their main purpose was procreation—to carry on the family name and legacy.

This stands in stark contrast to marriages today, especially in American culture. Our culture defines love as infatuation, not commitment. Relationships ebb and flow with fickle emotions, and marriages seem to occur primarily for the wedding rather than for a lifelong commitment. Divorces aren't whispered about because of shame; they're actually celebrated with parties. And now, it's not surprising to discover that a couple who live and have children together aren't married at all.

Both eras of marriage pose issues and seem to miss the real definition of love—a deliberate choice to commit yourself to someone else forever (as Christ has done His church), regardless of changing circumstances or emotions. Scripture also describes love:

> Love is patient, love is kind and is not jealous; love does not brag and is not arrogant, does not act unbecomingly; it does not seek its own, is not provoked, does not take into account a wrong

suffered, does not rejoice in unrighteousness, but rejoices with the truth; bears all things, believes all things, hopes all things, endures all things. Love never fails …[112]

Spouses who apply these truths in their marriages are those deserving honor, both in New Testament times and today. **Young women** didn't have **to love their husbands** in order to remain married or fulfill their marital duties. But those who did revealed their love for God and stood as a crowns for their husbands, worth far more than jewels.[113]

Loving their husbands was also one way **young women** loved **their children,** another trait that revealed spiritual maturity and commitment to Christ. The grammatical structure of this sentence in Greek is literally, "train the younger husband-loving to be child-loving…"[114] This means, among other things, that loving their husbands was first priority in a family setting, followed by loving their children.

By loving husbands first and foremost, **young women** reflected God's design and taught their children what real love is by giving them a living example. Putting children first and/or loving them more than spouses created serious problems in the homes of Cretan society, just as it does today. One thing to remember is that children are an active, daily part of life for a season; marriage is forever. Putting children first while neglecting one's marriage is a complete reversal of God's design and actually harms the children, both temporarily and in the long run. Children raised in homes like this tend to grow up thinking the world is about them, which detaches them from both present- and spiritual-world realities. Such a warped perspective negatively influences all their relationships and pursuits in life, not the least of which is their future marriage, for they have little concept of what a healthy marriage looks like.

Loving children involves more than showing kind affection for them. It means making persistent choices to put God's ideals into action—

prioritizing marriage, implementing discipline, revealing grace and love in every decision, teaching truth … basically, living out genuine faith in ways children can see and hopefully incorporate into their own lives as they grow. The best way to love children is to constantly show them Jesus and proclaim His gospel, first in word and then in deed.

One final note: just as he did in his instruction for elders, Paul recognizes that family comes first in the list of earthly relationships and priorities. We can accomplish all kinds of spiritual feats for the kingdom of God on paper, but if we achieve them while our families struggle and suffer from lack of our involvement, it's all for naught. The world offers many distractions, and Satan himself loves to disrupt and break up families, for he knows the disturbing effect that has on society as a whole. Choosing to believe the gospel and put God first means prioritizing what He does, and in this world, that list begins with family.

Young women, like elders and older men previously, are **to be sensible.** The same Greek word is used in all three cases (*sophron*) and, again, means to be self-controlled and sober-minded, able to restrain impulses as we filter them through the gospel. In regard to **young women,** "this was the cardinal virtue that defined the modest wife; it was to manifest itself above all in dignified conduct characterized by restraint of the passions and urges that might jeopardize fidelity to her husband."[115]

Yet we find another way to think about this in a different Pauline letter:

> We are destroying speculations and every lofty thing raised up against the knowledge of God, and we are taking every thought captive to the obedience of Christ.[116]

To be sensible means to take "every thought captive to the obedience of Christ." Lies and sinful thoughts pop into our heads; we're fallen, broken people even as God actively sanctifies us through the power of the Holy Spirit. But these thoughts and impulses aren't sins in themselves. Rather, our opportunity for sin (or further sanctification) lies in our response to them. **Young women** were **to be sensible** and take any sinful thought or urge under the control of the Holy Spirit—letting Him, not our fleshly desires, take charge.

To be sensible naturally leads to the next trait expected of younger women: to be **pure.** Purity in this context means to be chaste, which "hints at the sexual constraint aspects of self-control, although it also refers to fidelity in one's relationship with God."[117] Oh, what a distinction purity would make in the defiled Cretan culture! Even religious Jews had a horrendous history of infidelity to God.

Unfortunately, infidelity is a familiar concept weaved throughout Scripture, particularly in regard to Israel's gross lack of faithfulness to God. He chose Israel to proclaim His salvation to the world. Instead, they turned their backs on Him and prostituted themselves to other nations' false gods.

> My people consult their wooden idol, and their diviner's wand informs them; for a spirit of harlotry has led them astray, and they have played the harlot, departing from their God.[118]

Very few times throughout Israel's entire history can they be described as pure. Instead of serving God, who displayed His truth and might through incredible miracles and faithfulness, they chose other nations and their worthless idols:

> Their idols are silver and gold, the work of man's hands. They have mouths, but they cannot speak; they have eyes, but they cannot see; they have ears, but they cannot hear; they have noses, but they cannot smell; they have hands, but they cannot feel; they have feet, but they cannot walk; they cannot make a sound with their throat. Those who make them will become like them, everyone who trusts in them.[119]

Young women (and anyone else who claimed the name of Christ), chose the only true and living God over empty idols and fleshly temptations. They strove **to be pure** in their faithfulness to Him, which, of course, is but a reflection of His preceding and unwavering faithfulness to them.

In his instruction for younger women, Paul began with family priorities, moved to faithfulness in heart and conduct, and now continues to daily life expectations. **Older women** were also to train **young women** to be **workers at home** and **kind.** Some argue these two traits should be interpreted together, based on their construction in Greek, which would mean to "fulfill their household duties well."[120] Taken separately, **workers at home** would mean to be efficient at managing household duties, and **kind** would "indicate a lack of irritability in light of the nagging demands of mundane and routine household chores."[121] Regardless, **young women** were to perform their domestic responsibilities diligently and with a pleasant spirit.

Gender roles weren't a hot topic then as they are today. Both men and women performed specific roles within society and rarely questioned them. If a woman ventured outside her role, "she would have been thought selfish and decadent," not courageous and forward-thinking.[122] While it was absolutely the role of women to run their households, they were also engaged in activities and pursuits outside the home, including church ministries.[123] Some admittedly viewed women as property and treated them as slaves, but Christianity held women in honor and appreciation, certainly reflecting God's heart.

The intent of our passage, however, is far more about the *manner* in which responsibilities were fulfilled than the actual duties themselves. Things need to get done, as they have since the beginning of time. But Christians, especially women in this context, have the opportunity to make such work beautiful by the spirit in which they go about it. This, of course, is just another way the gospel is made beautiful when put into practice. By being

kind and having pleasant attitudes even during the most mundane of tasks, we showcase Christ and make Him that much more appealing to the world around us.

The last specific instruction for **young women** is to be **subject to their own husbands so that the word of God will not be dishonored.** We've already explored how being *subject* is not synonymous with being *slaves*, but is rather an opportunity to support, encourage, and follow a man who loves a woman sacrificially and gives anything and everything to help her shine in Christ. A wife's supportive position to her husband is constant, not dependent on him first fulfilling his God-given position. Wives have a unique and powerful position in marriage to sanctify it (or make it holy) by their obedience to God and His design of marriage. Even wives of unbelieving husbands hold this influence.[124] This marital posture, then, not only benefits the marriage, but also honors **the word of God.**

On the contrary, by standing against one's husband instead of standing with him in humility, a wife is guilty of dishonoring the word of God. The word for **dishonored** here is *blasphemeo* and is generally translated as blaspheming. It's as serious as it sounds. Bringing discord to marriage by not fulfilling proper roles is blasphemous, slanderous, and discrediting to God's Word. How could that be? Is God being overdramatic? Not at all, and here's why: as Christians, our lives reflect Christ. The radiance and purity of that reflection depends on our behavior, lifestyle, and actions—how they mirror and are motivated by the gospel.

If we reflect God's Word well, it is adorned and honored in our lives and in the lives of those around us. If we reflect it poorly via disobedience or other poor choices, we dishonor God and discredit His Word. We basically make Him a liar (which, we've already seen, is impossible because He cannot lie) by claiming we believe the gospel and then living its antithesis. That's why it's so dangerous for Christians to exemplify poor behavior and immoral lifestyles. It can cast doubt on the actuality of an individual's salvation, it causes the world to see hypocrisy, makes the gospel hideous to them, snuffs out any of their prior interest in God, and dishonors the very word on which we claim to base our lives and eternal destinies.

Our actions matter because they correspond with what we claim to believe. Genuine belief demands actions that harmonize with it. Otherwise, our words are but dangerous lip service that accomplish nothing but blasphemy and slander. **Older women** were empowered and encouraged to teach **young women** all these truths so their lives would honor **the word of God**, not blaspheme or discredit it.

LIKEWISE URGE THE YOUNG MEN TO BE SENSIBLE

Did Paul get a hand cramp when he got to this part? All the other gender/age groups were allotted a minimum of five instructions or exhortations to bring honor to God's Word in their lives; **young men** receive one. Since it's probably reasonable to assume that younger men weren't somehow immune to the depravity of Cretan society, let's explore this a bit further.

Most likely, this is Titus' category. Thus, he was most tuned in to the needs, struggles, and challenges that **young men** in Cretan society faced in that day and age. Paul knew this, and by keeping this instruction brief, was likely empowering Titus as a leader even more. The underlying message would perhaps be something like, "You're a young man facing all the same pressures and temptations as other young men. I trust you to teach them how to live according to God and His Word, both by word and example."

Another consideration is that, while the instruction is simple, it's deep. Most of its mass lies far below the surface of an initial glimpse. Like **older women** were to teach **young women,** Titus was to **urge young men to**

be sensible. Urge here is the same Greek word used in the first chapter of Titus, in which the elders were to **exhort** believers in sound doctrine. It means to encourage, summon, beseech, strengthen, and teach, all of which Titus was to do in helping other **young men** live out the gospel in their lives.

Sensible is the same root word as all our other encounters in this book so far.[125] Its meaning is complex, including all the points we've already discussed: being cool-headed and rational in any circumstance, showing measured restraint rather than acting on fleshly impulses, taking every thought captive by the truth, and allowing the Holy Spirit to be in control.

To be **sensible** is to master oneself, and this applies particularly to **young men.** Mastering oneself includes but is not limited to: recognizing worldly impulses and distinguishing them from the Spirit's, purposefully rejecting said impulses, intentionally embracing truth and the Spirit's guidance, and doing so immediately in any and every situation. Examples of such self-mastery include "the control of temper and tongue, of ambition and avarice, and especially of bodily appetites, including sexual urges, so that young men remain committed to the unalterable Christian standard of chastity before marriage and fidelity after it."[126]

Young men, including Titus, were **to be sensible** by mastering themselves—a discipline profoundly absent from Cretan society but ever present in a Christian's life.

IN ALL THINGS SHOW YOURSELF TO BE AN EXAMPLE OF GOOD DEEDS, WITH PURITY IN DOCTRINE, DIGNIFIED, SOUND IN SPEECH WHICH IS BEYOND REPROACH, SO THAT THE OPPONENT WILL BE PUT TO SHAME, HAVING NOTHING BAD TO SAY ABOUT US.

Paul makes a slight switch here from talking solely about **young men** to addressing Titus directly.[127] While Titus was included in the **young men** category, he was also distinct because of his position of leadership within the church. In addition to urging others to be sensible, he was also **to be an example** for them and the rest of the church body in Crete.

His example was first to be **of good deeds.** Again, our actions, lifestyles, and choices matter. They reflect God and His Word and also influence others either for or against Him. Titus stood in a particularly weighty position of influence in the church, so people watched him closely. Even more distinct were his **good deeds** against the backdrop of the false teachers "who deny God (whom they claim to worship) by their works and are disqualified from any good work."[128] Titus' actions aligned with his beliefs—a simple yet intense mark of integrity that should describe every Christian's life.

The Greek in the next part (**with purity in doctrine, dignified, sound in speech which is beyond reproach**) is a bit complicated to translate. The NASB is a strict translation and provides readers with the closest exact rendition to the individual Greek terms, word for word. This leaves the readers the opportunity to study and deduce correct interpretations on their own. Other translations implement a bit of further explanation, giving readers more the intended thought than the literal interpretation.

Many translate this part as "in your teaching show integrity, dignity, and sound speech that cannot be condemned,"[129] meaning Titus' teaching should be pure, dignified, and sound. Others, like the NASB, distinguish each word/phrase by its own merit, allowing the reader to feel the frustration and lack of clarity in Greek syntax. The majority of commentators agree that **purity in doctrine, dignified, sound in speech which is beyond reproach** refer to Titus' *teaching*, both in content and delivery methods, *not* in his example of good deeds (even though his good deeds should always reflect solid teaching).[130]

Paul instructed Titus to teach **with purity in doctrine,** which stands in direct opposition to the false leaders and their ulterior motives. In Greek, this literally means "be without corruption," giving us insight into the motives of his teaching, not the specific content.[131] While rebellious men taught for their own benefit, Titus was to be pure in his motives and delivery when teaching the gospel. A teacher in the church "is always faced with certain temptations to demonstrate one's own cleverness and to seek to attract notice to oneself rather than to God's message."[132] Especially in a culture as depraved as Crete, Titus would've had ample opportunity to take advantage of the Cretan believers and puff himself up in power, status, and as a keeper of the truth. But **purity** demanded he remain blameless and humble in his position, seeking the good and growth of those in his charge first and foremost.

Dignity, or seriousness, refers to the manner in which Titus delivered his teaching.[133] In essence, "this quality is meant to provide Titus' teaching with the accent of respectability that will distance it from the opponents' rambling arguments (1:10-11; 3:9) and disarm any critics outside the church before they get started."[134] It wouldn't bode well for Titus to allow emotions to dictate how he delivered the gospel message to Cretans. Being (righteously) upset and broken over their sin would be commendable, but allowing himself to be carried away by such emotions to the point he preached out of anger or spite would cause more harm than good. Rather, remaining cool-headed and deliberate would enable him to teach proactively, not reactively to what others were doing.

Some scholars believe **sound in speech** refers to the nature of Titus' teaching rather than its content. This would interpret **sound in speech** as "a healthy, well-thought-out and attractively delivered presentation of the Christian gospel," not the gospel itself.[135] Others consider that **speech** (the Greek word *logos*) has been used elsewhere in Titus solely as the gospel message, and interpret it likewise. Regardless of specific viewpoint, the heart of these verses remains the same: Titus was to live with integrity and purity, as an example of the gospel he was teaching.

Paul once again uses the phrase **beyond reproach.** This term differs slightly from the first two uses in chapter one, which are translated "*above reproach,*" but the idea is the same. The gospel message and Titus' delivery of it, both in word and deed, were to be blameless, **so that the opponent will be put to shame, having nothing bad to say about us.**

The **opponent** here is vague because of its singular tense. The **rebellious men** of chapter one were undoubtedly plural, so we're not positive who Paul has in mind here. Some commentators believe he is speaking of Satan, others think it's a singular representation of a group of opponents.[136] Or it could just be a vague symbol for anyone who opposes the gospel and its workers. Fortunately, the specific identity of the **opponent** isn't all that important, because it doesn't change Paul's point—**the opponent will be put to shame** by the gospel and Titus' example of it.

Put to shame does not mean Paul wishes the opponent demise, humiliation, or disgrace. Rather, it plays off opponents being **silenced** in chapter one, with their message and reputation discredited in the community when compared to the truth of the gospel.[137] When the gospel's power is unleashed in the teaching and lives of church leaders, any and all opposition crumbles, **having nothing bad to say about** those who believe it.

Titus led the Cretan church as he followed Christ with his whole being— his intellectual assentation to the gospel, example of the good deeds it inspires, and dignified preaching of it to silence any and all who oppose.

URGE BONDSLAVES TO BE SUBJECT TO THEIR OWN MASTERS IN EVERYTHING, TO BE WELL-PLEASING, NOT ARGUMENTATIVE, NOT PILFERING, BUT SHOWING ALL GOOD FAITH SO THAT THEY WILL ADORN THE DOCTRINE OF GOD OUR SAVIOR IN EVERY RESPECT.

Having addressed all adult gender and age combinations, Paul now provides instruction to those with the status of bondslaves. The term

bondslaves here (*doulous*) is the same term Paul used to identify himself in reference to God in the introduction of this letter. Again, we're mistaken to hold the same impression of slaves in New Testament times as we do former slavery in America. First-century slaves were indistinguishable in race, religion, and culture from their masters, and often even willingly became slaves so they could boost their own societal status when they earned their freedom. While there were admittedly some slaves in awful conditions, a good many were "in apprentice or indentured relationships, domestic workers, and some who held high government office."[138] Thus, we shouldn't allow ourselves to become distracted by the presuppositions we bring to the text. Paul isn't dealing with the morality of slavery in this passage, as much as we'd prefer he did. The point of this specifically targeted group is to show the possibility and expectation of the gospel being lived out beautifully in everyone's life, regardless of societal class.

Just as the gospel welcomed people from all races (not just Judaism as it did prior to Christ), it also welcomed people from every social class. Christ made access to God equal-opportunity for all who would accept Him, meaning church congregations were a mix of genders, races, and social statuses. This is one seriously radiant aspect of the gospel, and one striking glimpse into what heaven will be like. In his vision of Revelation, the apostle John says:

> ... I heard the voice of many angels around the throne and the living creatures and the elders; and the number of them was myriads of myriads, and thousands of thousands, saying with a loud voice, "Worthy is the Lamb that was slain to receive power and riches and wisdom and might and honor and glory and blessing." And every created thing which is in heaven and on the earth and under the earth and on the sea, and all things in them, I heard saying, "To Him who sits on the throne, and to the Lamb, be blessing and honor and glory and dominion forever and ever."[139]

Our minds are incapable of comprehending God's glory, but we will spend eternity basking in it, right alongside people from every tribe, tongue, people, and nation.[140] Social castes don't exist in heaven; neither should they exist in the part of God's family currently residing on earth. We are to see one another as God does—loved by Him, saved by His grace, and an equal part of His family. Christians are to look past physical, educational, and socioeconomic classes, because that's exactly what God has done for us.

Good or bad, the position of **bondslave** was a reality back then, but their status did not encroach upon their ability to receive salvation and live out the gospel from which they derived it. For **bondslaves**, part of living out the gospel was **to be subject to their own masters in everything.** This command echoes the one given to young women in being **subject to their own husbands**, for the same Greek word, *hypotasso,* is also used to communicate the cooperative yielding of **bondslaves** to their masters. A word of clarity, though: **bondslaves** and **young women** were not expected to serve in the same capacity. Wives were not slaves to their husbands. The two do, however, share a similar role of deliberate compliance to the people God placed as leaders in their lives.

Bondslaves were expected to submit to their masters, even apart from religion. Christian **bondslaves**, however, like Christians in general, had higher standards. Believing the gospel meant not just obedience, but obedience done well—**well-pleasing, not argumentative,** and **not pilfering.**

These three instructions are pretty straightforward. **Well-pleasing** encompasses the rest of the expectations, just as **above reproach** covered all of an elder's qualifications. Among other things, it means they were to be agreeable and exemplify a positive attitude in their duties, as well as having a godly attitude when they interacted with people. Attitude makes a big difference in every relationship and circumstance. Consider having a colleague who technically does everything required of him, but is absolutely miserable to be around. Such a negative presence would be draining to you, other collaborators, customers, vendors, etc.

While **bondslaves** were hardly considered leaders in society, they definitely impacted the homes they served in. Christian **bondslaves** had a unique opportunity to display Christ by the attitude in which they carried out their responsibilities every day. Paul touches on this thought in Colossians:

> Slaves, in all things obey those who are your masters on earth, not with external service, as those who merely please men, but with sincerity of heart, fearing the Lord. Whatever you do, do your work heartily, as for the Lord rather than for men, knowing that from the Lord you will receive the reward of the inheritance. It is the Lord Christ whom you serve.[141]

While Christian **bondslaves** served their human masters, their service and conduct thereof was, in reality, offered to Christ. Their earthly work gave them an opportunity to invest in heavenly rewards, which they would receive in full if they were diligent to live out the gospel in a way that made it shine.

This is especially heavy in light of their situation and status. While many slaves enjoyed satisfying lives and were provided for (housing, meals, clothing, etc.), others did suffer in their positions, making **well-pleasing** behavior rather difficult. But it was possible, and the result was deep— against an ugly "system of bondage, the Christian slave's devotion to the gospel and resulting godly attitudes and actions serve to make attractive in an unparalleled way the ultimate freedom that is only realized in Christ."[142]

Part of being **well-pleasing,** both to God and their human masters, was to be agreeable, **not argumentative.** This directive "has to do with disputing what someone says, directly contradicting, or, even worse, opposing to the point of refusing to do what one is supposed to."[143] Part of being **subject to their own masters in everything** meant obedience without talking back. Just as they wouldn't (or shouldn't) talk back to God or argue with Him over His commands, they wouldn't talk back to their human masters.

The next mandate was for servants to be honest, **not pilfering** or stealing. This was a real temptation for slaves back then, for they "were often entrusted with buying goods and also often had a degree of private ownership."[144] While he wasn't a servant, Judas Iscariot, one of Jesus' disciples, did this. He was in charge of managing the funds for Jesus and His ministry, and instead of being honest, he stole from them.[145] Money has been a temptation since the beginning of time, and Jesus recognized its alluring pull when He said,

> "No one can serve two masters; for either he will hate the one and love the other, or he will be devoted to one and despise the other. You cannot serve God and wealth."[146]

Bondslaves, then, were to handle money with integrity. As servants of Christ primarily, they were to conduct themselves in a manner worthy of Him, which absolutely included not stealing from their masters.

Lastly, **bondslaves** were to show **all good faith.** This phrase is difficult when examined in the Greek, but it essentially means "to show that they can be fully trusted."[147] Trust can be difficult to solidify yet easy to break. Finding a trustworthy friend or colleague is a breath of fresh air, for we can let down our guards around them. The same could be said of **bondslaves** back then. Masters would undoubtedly relish having servants whom they could trust (especially in such a conniving society), having been freed from the burden of worrying over and micro-managing their conduct.

All the aforementioned requirements for **bondslaves** held a powerful purpose: **so that they will adorn the doctrine of God our Savior in**

every respect. This statement, while given specifically in reference to servants, sums up the purpose behind all the other groupings' actions and behaviors discussed previously. A Christian's actions either beautify or blacken the gospel as it's seen through the eyes of the world. Another way of thinking about it is that the gospel message "will be judged by the behavior of Christians."[148]

God never explains why He chooses to use us as conduits of His gospel. He certainly didn't need us; if anything, we do more harm for the expansion of the gospel than we do good. But in His omniscient sovereignty, He purposed for us to be His hands, feet, and heart to the world. We represent Him, and all our thoughts, words, actions, and reactions reflect Him. That's why it's so important for us to live righteously; by doing so, we **adorn** or make attractive not only His doctrine, but His very person.

GROUP STUDY

INTRODUCTION

Beauty ignites an eternal longing in our souls.

Beauty is one of the most sought-after, yet elusive, entities in all of creation. We crave it—both to be beautiful and to fill our lives with beauty via relationships and possessions. We enjoy it, whether we're soaking up sunshine along the coast or gazing down from a mountain peak higher than the clouds. And we try to hold onto it with photographs capturing our favorite views or extensive surgeries trying to unwind the clock's aging influence on our bodies. But beauty is fleeting; at least, in the way the world defines it.

- How does the world define beauty?

- What is one of the most beautiful things you've ever seen?

  - Why was it so beautiful?

THE WORD

Beauty entices us to pursue it, largely because it awakens a deeper longing within our souls for something more ... and something permanent. One pure and eternal example of beauty that our souls long to access is the gospel. Its radiance is irresistible, its content incapable of disappointing. And we, as Christians, are tasked to reveal it to the world.

Paul knew the impact a believer's life has on the world's perception of the gospel. Against the debauchery of Cretan culture, the gospel would shine brilliantly and compel others to draw near, if only the church would live it out in their lifestyles and conduct. In typical Pauline style, he provides lists that particular groups of people were to embrace in their pursuit of exemplifying the gospel:

> Older men are to be temperate, dignified, sensible, sound in faith, in love, in perseverance. (Titus 2:2)

> Older women likewise are to be reverent in their behavior, not malicious gossips nor enslaved to much wine, teaching what is good, so that they may encourage the young women ... (Titus 2:3)

> Young women were to "love their husbands, to love their children, to be sensible, pure, workers at home, kind, being subject to their own husbands, so that the word of God will not be dishonored." (Titus 2:4-5)

> Young men were "to be sensible" in all that entailed. (Titus 2:6)

> Titus was to "speak the things which are fitting for sound doctrine," and "to be an example of good deeds, with purity in doctrine, dignified, sound in speech which is beyond reproach." (Titus 2:1, 7-8)

> Bondslaves were "to be subject to their own masters in everything, to be well-pleasing, not argumentative, not pilfering, but showing all good faith so that they will adorn the doctrine of God our Savior in every respect." (Titus 2:9-10)

- What groupings of people did Paul specify?

- What behaviors are repeated throughout the lists?

- In what ways are these significant to individuals, families, the church, and communities when observed?

- Which categorical list is shortest?

  - Why is that?

- What role were older women to play in the church community?

  - Who benefited from that? How so?

- In what ways are roles (gender included) an opportunity to thrive in our faith and relationships?

- What was the relationship between all these actions and the gospel/doctrine? (Titus 2:5,10)

APPLY

We each identify with a particular group in this passage. We can also identify with the purpose of their corresponding behaviors—adorning the Word of God with our actions. We have the unique position of representing God to the world, sharing His good news not only verbally, but also in the way we live.

> Let your light shine before men in such a way that they may see your
> good works, and glorify your Father who is in heaven.
> Jesus, Matthew 5:16

> For just as the body without the spirit is dead, so also faith without
> works is dead.
> James, James 2:26

- How would you describe the general morality of the culture surrounding you—work, community, town, etc.?

    - In what ways is it easy to stand out as a Christian living righteously?

- In what ways is it difficult to stand out as a Christian living righteously?

- What one area in your life (habit, tendency, etc.) needs work to make the gospel shine brighter (and more beautifully) in and through you?

- How can you work on it this week?

WEEK FOUR
TITUS 2:11-15

PERSONAL BIBLE STUDY QUESTIONS

1. What has appeared? (2:11)

2. Who is salvation offered to? (2:11)

3. What does salvation instruct Christians to do? (2:12)

    a)

    b)

    c)

    d)

    e)

4. What do believers look for as we live out those instructions? (2:13)

    a)

    b)

5. What did Christ's sacrifice do for those who believe? (2:14)

6. What should a Christian's perspective be in regard to good deeds? (2:14)

   a) Do you think this is how the church views them? Why or why not?

   b) Would you define your perspective of good deeds this way? Why or why not?

7. How was Titus supposed to use these truths in his ministry? (2:15)

   a)

   b)

   c)

COMMENTARY

> For the grace of God has appeared, bringing salvation to all men,
> instructing us to deny ungodliness and worldly desires and to live
> sensibly, righteously and godly in the present age, looking for the
> blessed hope and the appearing of the glory of our great God and
> Savior, Christ Jesus, who gave Himself for us to redeem us from
> every lawless deed, and to purity for Himself a people for His
> own possession, zealous for good deeds. These things speak and
> exhort and reprove with all authority. Let no one disregard you.
> Titus 2:11-15

Motivation. It's the force that drives us to accomplish our goals. It's a key
factor in determining the guilt of a suspect in a criminal case. It's an
occupation for speakers, often corresponding with self-help-inspired
literature. It keeps us focused. It fuels adrenaline as we pursue a task. Above
all, it's the reason behind everything we do, everything we think, and
everything we say.

Many people approach the Christian life with tainted motivations.
Reasons for initially accepting Christ are almost always motivated by
selfish gain—going to heaven, helping break an addiction, improving the
quality of life, attaining inner peace, penance for guilt over an action or
behavior … the list is endless. Many use the gospel as a means to an end,
not an end itself to the glory of God.

Unfortunately, such deficient motivations carry through to daily life and
the way we live out our faith. We choose "good" behaviors and actions in
order to boost egos, improve our self-image, or even to try to earn God's
favor. It's as if people think they receive salvation by grace but keep
salvation through their good works.[149] Technically, we can accomplish
"good works" even with erroneous motivations. But any rewards those

works win us will be shallow, and we'll receive those rewards only in this life, not in eternity.

Paul's instruction thus far may have seemed overwhelming for the Cretan believers as they learned the truths from Titus. Indeed, they'd be left in a depressed state if they bore the weight of such requirements solely on their shoulders. To avoid that misunderstanding, Paul explains the motivation behind a believer's obedience to God—the reason they should adorn the gospel with their lives …

FOR THE GRACE OF GOD HAS APPEARED

For is yet another conjunction word connecting two of Paul's thoughts. In this case, he is connecting his behavioral directives of verses one through ten with the motivations behind them. The Cretans were not to obey simply for the sake of obedience, though frankly, that would've been enough. (If the Creator of the universe mandates something, we should absolutely obey.) Paul instead is reminding Titus to teach them the theology beyond the instruction, for he wants them to view everything— including their obedient lifestyles—within the framework of the gospel of Jesus Christ.

Why should they make the gospel beautiful by living above reproach? First, because **the grace of God has appeared.** As we discussed previously, grace is the unmerited favor of God bestowed on us through the sacrifice of Jesus Christ. Our souls should rot in the eternal decay our depravity deserves. But in His grace, God reaches down, rescues us, and adopts us into His reality—into truth. This is based on nothing we have done, but rather, in spite of all we have done against Him. Totally unnecessary, nearly unfathomable. That's grace. We don't deserve it and never will, but we can accept it and savor it as we wait to be ushered into His unimpeded glory.

The agent of this **grace** was Jesus Christ. Indeed, we cannot experience grace apart from Jesus, because He's the only one who could pay its incomprehensible price. While we note representations of grace throughout the Old Testament, as strong as they are, they only foreshadow the intensity of grace as it was manifested in Jesus Christ, who **appeared** at just the right time.

In the introduction to this letter, Paul touched on the concept of time by declaring that God **at the proper time manifested, even His word.** God exists outside of time—a thousand years in His sight are like merely a day.[150] He created time for our benefit, chooses to operate within it, and at the exact right moment in history, sent His Son into the world to put His gospel plan in place.

When Paul writes that **the grace of God has appeared,** he means in part that it came at a specific, definitive time. It didn't operate like a big bang theory and simply show up with no rhyme or reason. God methodically orchestrated the manifestation of His gospel throughout the history of the world, culminating it at the birth of Christ in that lowly Bethlehem stable.

Pure lifestyles among Cretan believers, then, were first to be motivated by **the grace of God** that had **appeared** through Jesus Christ. They received a staggering gift that was sorely undeserved, and their response (after acceptance) was to reflect the Giver with their blameless lifestyles. Such conformity was made substantially easier—even enjoyable—against a backdrop of eternal gratitude. While they could never earn grace or pay God back for it, they could show their profound appreciation by living in ways that mirrored the gift extended to them, especially when the gift resulted in the eternal security of their souls.

... BRINGING SALVATION TO ALL MEN

The result of grace realized is **salvation,** the crown jewel of the gospel message. **Salvation** means to be brought to life in Christ and secured in

His everlasting future. It's redemption, rescue, new life, freedom, light, enlightenment, transformation, refuge, an anchor for the soul, truth, discovery, justification, sanctification, peace, joy, favor with God, unconditional approval, and hope that will never dim or fade away. Our souls were once dead because of our sin, which would've forever kept us from God. But now they are resuscitated and brought to life in Christ:

> God, who gives life to the dead and calls into being that which does not exist.[151]

> And you were dead in your trespasses and sins, in which you formerly walked according to the course of this world, according to the prince of the power of the air, of the spirit that is now working in the sons of disobedience…But God, being rich in mercy, because of His great love with which He loved us, even when we were dead in our transgressions, made us alive together with Christ …[152]

> When you were dead in your transgressions and the uncircumcision of your flesh, He made you alive together with Him, having forgiven us all our transgressions.[153]

Salvation gives us life and gives our life purpose—to glorify God and enjoy Him forever.[154] It's not something we can earn (dead people can't do anything, certainly not bring themselves to life), but is rather a gift from God.

> For the wages of sin is death, but the free gift of God is eternal life in Christ Jesus our Lord.[155]

> For by grace you have been saved through faith; and that not of yourselves, it is the gift of God; not as a result of works, so that no one may boast.[156]

God initiates and accomplishes everything in salvation. People aren't even capable of seeking Him on their own; He puts a desire within their hearts and nurtures it to faith. How is salvation received? People obtain salvation when they respond in faith (the faith God imparted to their hearts) to the gospel—first by knowing it, then by believing and embracing it with their whole person.

The gospel: God's plan to rescue a spiritually dead, broken, condemned, and sin-enslaved world, giving eternal life and restoring it to peace with Him through the comprehensive and final sacrifice of Jesus Christ—who was born of a virgin, lived a sinless life, died on the cross, was buried, and rose again—bringing us to life in Him, adopting us into His family, and securing us in His glorious future.

> But what does it say? "The Word is near you, in your mouth and in your heart,"—that is, the word of faith which we are preaching, that if you confess with your mouth Jesus as Lord, and believe in your heart that God raised Him from the dead, you will be saved; for with the heart a person believes, resulting in righteousness, and with the mouth he confesses, resulting in salvation.[157]

By acknowledging their spiritual deadness, repenting of the sin that caused it, and accepting Christ's payment on their behalf, people receive salvation. And this salvation is available **to all men.**

All men means mankind as a whole, not the male gender only. Men and women, children and adults, slaves and free, poor and rich—all are included in salvation.

> For God so loved the world, that He gave His only begotten Son, that whoever believes in Him shall not perish, but have eternal life. For God did not send the Son into the world to judge the world, but that the world might be saved through Him.[158]

But just because it's offered doesn't mean all will accept salvation. Even though they've been presented with the gospel, some reject it and choose their opinions of eternity over God's truth:

> He came to His own, and those who were His own did not receive Him. But as many as received Him, to them He gave the right to become children of God, even to those who believe in His name.[159]

As long as we have breath, we have the opportunity to come to Christ in salvation. No one is beyond hope; no one is too far for God's grace to reach. God "desires all men to be saved and to come to the knowledge of the truth,"[160] and made it available to the whole world, despite knowing that not everyone would accept it.

Those who do accept **salvation** are changed, and their lives begin to reflect it. Paul encourages Titus to remind the Cretans of this very truth. The church's actions and godly lifestyles were a response to the **salvation** they graciously received from God, not a requirement to achieve or sustain it.

INSTRUCTING US TO DENY UNGODLINESS AND WORLDLY DESIRES

God's **grace** in **bringing salvation to all men** instructs **us to deny ungodliness and worldly desires.** With this statement, Paul continues showing us that **salvation** is to motivate the way Titus and Cretan Christians lived their lives. First, salvation motivates by **instructing** them **to deny ungodliness.** God doesn't save us and say, "Cool, welcome to the family. I'll see you when you get to heaven one day." That'd be ridiculous! Eternal life doesn't begin when we die; it begins the moment we accept Christ. From that moment on, we are raised to life and immediately begin to live it out. The gospel isn't just the means of receiving eternal life. It also instructs us how to live it in the here and now.

Instructing, here, is not a complicated word. It's the Greek word *paideuo* and means to teach or train.[161] Education in New Testament times was highly revered, greatly sought after, and widely practiced. Greeks believed education produced virtue.[162] They spent countless hours philosophizing and discussing anything they could think of, and Paul is no doubt playing off such a mindset in the way he pens these words.[163] Therefore, "the past appearance of God's grace is seen to be presently effective in the human sphere in an educational sense."[164]

The gospel instructs **us** (the church, people who have accepted Christ as their Lord and Savior) in many ways, including **to deny ungodliness.** Sanctification (or the process of being made holy or Christ-like) involves two movements. First, we must move away from sin, and then we must move toward godliness. A shallow comparison is like breaking a habit. People who want to quit smoking not only say no to cigarettes, but they often also say yes to something in its place—gum, temporary nicotine patches, exercise, a healthy diet, etc. They are essentially replacing something bad with something good. The same can be said with sanctification. Sanctification requires us to replace sinful habits and behaviors with actions and attitudes that honor Christ in and through our lives.

This replacement occurs initially when Christians **deny** harmful behaviors. To **deny,** *arneomai,* is also translated to renounce, to turn from, and to reject. Christians must actively and purposefully say no to any desire that does not glorify God.

If a behavior doesn't reflect godliness, it likely exemplifies **ungodliness.** This word in Greek is *asebeia* and it "calls to mind idolatry and associated wicked practices, depicts life in the world as basically irreligious, totally apart from God, determined by unbelief."[165] Basically, **ungodliness** encompasses everything Christians should not demonstrate in their lives. A Christian's life is marked by Christ; a godless individual is marked by the world.

Since believers know only **ungodliness and worldly desires** before coming to Christ, they have to adopt a whole new perspective in order **to deny** them.

> For those who are according to the flesh set their minds on the things of the flesh, but those who are according to the Spirit, the things of the Spirit. For the mind set on the flesh is death, but the mind set on the Spirit is life and peace, because the mind set on the flesh is hostile toward God; for it does not subject itself to the law of God, for it is not even able to do so, and those who are in the flesh cannot please God.[166]

Before Christ, people are dead in spirit and alive in **worldly desires**. After salvation, they are alive in spirit and need to put **worldly desires** to death by **deny**ing them. **Worldly desires** belong "to the human society that ignores or despises God,"[167] of which Crete stood in all its arrogant shame. As a whole, they allowed their flesh (or ungodly impulses) to determine their conduct and pursuits. Self-restraint was foreign to them, as was living by any kind of moral standard. If they felt like it, they did it, not caring one bit about the moral repercussions of their decisions.

Cretan Christians were to stand out from their society in a diligent effort **to deny ungodliness and worldly desires.** Having been freed from the chains of the world and its narrow view of life, they were now able to pursue their eternal lives in ways that honored God.

What does this look like practically? It varies for everyone—Cretan and modern Christians alike. First, we need to evaluate our lives with spiritual magnifying glasses, which is best accomplished when done in the context of prayer and in accountability relationships. What areas hinder our relationship with God? Do we lack peace? Joy? Trust? Contentment? What are our priorities? What are known, habitual sins? What spiritual discipline do we lack? What do we desire? By poking around our lives through a spiritual lens and asking God to reveal areas of concern, we can target any aspects that are still marked by the world and need change.

Second, we need to get practical. After identifying areas of concern, we need to think of ways we can actively combat or deny them. If we have a problem with gossip, one practical step we can take is to say only nice, edifying, and wonderful things about people (without sarcasm). Or be silent. If we struggle with an addiction, we can join a support group and get an accountability partner. Regardless of how **ungodliness and worldly desires** manifest themselves, we need to take practical action to reject them.

Lastly, we need to be persistent, committed, and motivated by the right things (i.e., the gospel). When we purge sin from our lives, we do so out of profound gratitude for the gospel and what Christ accomplished on our behalf. When we think of what He's done and what He endured for us, silly things like jealousy or anger become manageable. But we have to keep at it, continuing to preach the gospel to ourselves until it becomes louder than the former desires of our flesh.

AND TO LIVE SENSIBLY, RIGHTEOUSLY AND GODLY IN THE PRESENT AGE

In their pursuit of holy living, Titus and the Cretan Christians were to say no to **ungodliness and worldly desires** and begin **to live sensibly, righteously, and godly in the present age.** Again, getting rid of bad things without replacing them with good things leaves a void and makes it much easier to fall back into prior sinful habits. But when believers say yes to holiness, they take active measures to become Christ-like and shine His gospel to the world.

> If indeed you have heard Him and have been taught in Him, just as truth is in Jesus, that, in reference to your former manner of

life, *you lay aside the old self, which is being corrupted in accordance with the lusts of deceit,* and that you be renewed in the spirit of your mind, and *put on the new self, which in the likeness of God* has been created in righteousness and holiness of the truth.[168]

After they "put aside the old self" by **denying ungodliness and worldly desires,** Cretan Christians were **to live sensibly.** This is the fifth time we've encountered this instruction in Paul's letter to Titus. The first was in reference to qualifications for elders (1:8), the second described what older men should strive for (2:2), the third was in reference to younger women (2:5), and the fourth was the sole direct instruction for younger men (2:6). Clearly, Cretan society struggled with living sensibly, and the Cretan church receives yet another reminder to adopt such a lifestyle in their pursuit of holiness.

So far in our discussion, **to live sensibly** has included being sober in thinking, dealings, and relationships; showing calculated restraint in everything, taking every thought captive to the gospel in obedience to Christ, and mastering oneself with utmost discipline. All these definitions are relevant in this particular context, with perhaps a slight emphasis on "prudence which has everything under perfect control, and which allows no passion or desire more than its proper place."[169] **To live sensibly** is not to live without temptations or worldly impulses, but to control them, not to be controlled by them.

To live **righteously,** or to put on righteousness in the place of **ungodliness,** means first to be in a right relationship with God in Christ and then "to live as righteous people, devoted to the service of what God declares to be right."[170] Another way of thinking of it is to live uprightly, to change once-sinful standards of behavior to God's standards of reverence and honor. Christ imparted His righteousness to us as part of His sacrifice on the cross. While Adam brought sin into the world, condemning everyone, Christ brought an offer of righteousness into the world, making right with God all who would believe:

For if by the transgression of the one, death reigned through the one, much more those who receive the abundance of grace and of the gift of righteousness will reign in life through the One, Jesus Christ. So then as through one transgression there resulted condemnation to all men, even so through one act of righteousness there resulted justification of life to all men. For as through the one man's disobedience the many were made sinners, even so through the obedience of the One the many will be made righteous. The Law came in so that the transgression would increase; but where sin increased, grace abounded all the more, so that, as sin reigned in death, even so grace would reign through righteousness to eternal life through Jesus Christ our Lord.[171]

We are made right with God the very moment we are saved, but we need to exercise our position in the way we live.

To complete the trifecta, **godly** living is added. To live **godly** is to live piously or devoted to God, which is the exact opposite of the **ungodliness** they were to deny. Paul is all about contrasts in this letter, putting the Cretans up against Christians living in their midst. By specifying these three virtues, he's actually "expressing three of the four cardinal virtues of Platonism-Stoicism" (highly regarded in New Testament times), though with a distinctly Christian twist.[172] With this final positive directive, he tells believers to live **godly** in a world, culture, and society that is incomprehensibly ungodly. Just as Christ was the light in a world consumed by darkness, Christians are to shine His light in a world continually dimmed by sin.

I have come as Light into the world, so that everyone who believes in Me will not remain in darkness.[173]

Then Jesus again spoke to them, saying, "I am the Light of the world; he who follows Me will not walk in the darkness, but will have the Light of life."[174]

… He who practices the truth comes to the Light, so that his deeds may be manifested as having been wrought in God.[175]

Let your light shine before men in such a way that they may see your good works, and glorify your Father who is in heaven.[176]

If we bear the name of God in Christ, we, in essence, glow with His Spirit, Who radiates in and through our lives. When we take it further and practice the truth we believe, particularly by being **godly**, we fuel the flame like gasoline on a fire.

In the present age once again refers to time. Just as **the grace of God has appeared** and did so at a particular time in history, this current age is also specific: Christ came and the church is waiting for Him to come again. This is known as dispensationalism in theological circles, which basically means that God has related to humanity in different ways throughout history, depending on which stage of the gospel was currently unfolding at the time. Those adhering to this view read "Old Testament Israel and the New Testament church as successive institutions in biblical history which reveal irreducible aspects of a multipurpose or multidimensional divine plan."[177] We, along with Cretan Christians, live in a peculiar era. The Old Testament and all its covenantal promises were fulfilled in Christ, whom we have accepted and in whom we place our faith. But the story isn't over. We're saved, but we await the culmination of our salvation (unhindered union with Jesus for all eternity). We're justified, but we wait to be comprehensibly justified (in our beings just as in our position before God). We are sanctified, but we wait for our sanctification to be fully manifested when we are present with Christ:

For now we see in a mirror dimly, but then face to face; now I know in part, but then I will know fully just as I also have been fully known.[178]

And just like good deeds and holy lifestyles, our present reality as Christians should always be motivated by the future reality awaiting us in Christ Jesus.

The **salvation** Christians received after **the grace of God has appeared** was to fuel the way they lived—putting off **ungodliness and worldly desires** in order to put on living **sensibly, righteously, and godly in this present age.**

LOOKING FOR THE BLESSED HOPE AND THE APPEARING OF THE GLORY OF OUR GREAT GOD AND SAVIOR, CHRIST JESUS

Faith is motivated by the gospel, which has past, present, and future implications. The gospel began before the creation of the world (it's not as if Adam and Eve caught God by surprise with their sin). It's first mention is in Genesis 3, and it continues to weave throughout the Old Testament as God prepares hearts for the coming Messiah. When the Messiah, Jesus Christ, came, He fulfilled all Old Testament prophecies about Himself, accomplished His mission by serving as the final and comprehensive sacrifice for our sins, and ascended to heaven and sits "at the right hand of God, who also intercedes for us."[179] When Christ ascended into heaven, He didn't leave us alone:

But the Helper, the Holy Spirit, whom the Father will send in My name, He will teach you all things, and bring to your remembrance all that I said to you.[180]

But I tell you the truth, it is to your advantage that I go away; for if I do not go away, the Helper will not come to you; but if I go, I will send Him to you.[181]

The Holy Spirit dwells in those who have accepted Christ—helping, guiding, correcting, interceding, gifting, encouraging, and empowering believers to live according to the gospel in which they have been called. The Spirit performs this role in the present until Christ comes again in the future. Therefore, Cretan believers, like those living today, were to be **looking for the blessed hope and the appearing of the glory of our great God and Savior, Christ Jesus.**

Definitions for the Greek word *prosdechomai* (**looking**) include to accept, allow, look for, receive, take, and wait for.[182] In the context of this verse, it is best regarded as "eagerly waiting for." Such language saturates the New Testament in reference to our posture for Christ's return:

> For our citizenship is in heaven, from which also we eagerly wait for a Savior, the Lord Jesus Christ; who will transform the body of our humble state into conformity with the body of His glory, by the exertion of the power that He has even to subject all things to Himself.[183]

> So Christ also, having been offered once to bear the sins of many, will appear a second time for salvation without reference to sin, to those who eagerly await Him.[184]

> Therefore do not go on passing judgment before the time, but wait until the Lord comes who will both bring to light the things hidden in the darkness and disclose the motives of men's hearts; and then each man's praise will come to him from God.[185]

Cretan believers were to anticipate Christ's return eagerly, because it promises to be even more amazing than the relationship they got to enjoy with Him on earth. Their lives were motivated both by what Christ had done and what He will do when He returns. The eternal life they'd begun to live will one day be fully realized, and this hope will be worth every trial, tribulation, setback, disappointment, ache, and sorrow experienced in their pursuit of Light in a darkened world. Their lives, then, should reflect their enthusiastic expectation of that day.

One further note on this point. Just as no one knew when Jesus would come the first time, no one knows when He will come again—"of that day or hour no one knows, not even the angels in heaven, nor the Son, but the Father alone."[186] That's one reason it's so important not just to know about His second coming, but to prepare for it. Jesus said to "be on the alert, then, for you do not know the day nor the hour," when He will return.[187] In other words, Jesus' second coming (like His first) serves as motivation for believers to live well and let the gospel shine in and through them. Because we don't know when He will come, it's our responsibility to remain alert and live as though that day could be today.

The first object of their eager anticipation is **the blessed hope** that would come. Paul mentioned **hope** previously in the introduction, when he revealed that the foundation of his apostleship is **the hope of eternal life.** His apostleship and ministry were grounded on and fueled by the **hope** (or fact) of eternal life. Now he encourages Titus and Cretan Christians to adhere to the same perspective, allowing **the blessed hope** to drive their lifestyle and behavioral choices. Again, **hope** isn't a wish or even a strong desire that something may be true. In Christ, **hope** is a guarantee, a promise that something will come about—in this case, Christ.

Blessed is a term like faith and hope in church circles; it's about lost its meaning due to overuse. We're blessed to have gotten a front-row parking spot just as we're blessed to be saved. Our houses, jobs, vehicles, clothes, financial security, mental stability, friendships, gym memberships, and anything else under the sun (the sun itself, for that matter) are all blessings from God. While all that can technically be true, it's an incomplete picture of what being **blessed** is truly about.

Blessed are the poor in spirit, for theirs is the kingdom of heaven. Blessed are those who mourn, for they shall be comforted. Blessed are the gentle, for they shall inherit the earth. Blessed are those who hunger and thirst for righteousness, for they shall be satisfied. Blessed are the merciful, for they shall receive mercy. Blessed are the pure in heart, for they shall see God. Blessed are the peacemakers, for they shall be called sons of God. Blessed are those who have been persecuted for the sake of righteousness, for theirs is the kingdom of heaven. Blessed are you when people insult you and persecute you, and falsely say all kinds of evil against you because of Me. Rejoice and be glad, for your reward in heaven is great …[188]

The word **blessed** literally means happy. "Someone has suggested that it might be put like this; this is the sort of man who is to be congratulated, this is the sort of man to be envied, for he alone is truly happy."[189] Not a fleeting happiness defined with emotions, but a deep happiness substantiated by the character of someone secure in their relationship with God.

Being **blessed**, then, is completely independent of circumstances, for someone can be happy even in the most grueling of outward situations. Rather, it reflects one's standing with God. If we are in Christ, we are in His favor and are thereby blessed. We may choose not to respond to our position of blessing appropriately, but we always have the ability to align our emotions with the truth of God's Word and our identities in Him.

What does **blessed hope** mean? Simply, it means the hope to come has God's full favor. It is something we yearn for with happiness, because it's a promise that brings more joy than we can ever fathom this side of heaven.

Along with **the blessed hope**, Cretan believers were to actively look for **the appearing of the glory of our great God and Savior, Christ Jesus.**

One day, at a time known only to God the Father, **Christ Jesus** will **appear** in all His glory. We're not given many details as to how He will return, but angels did give the original eleven disciples a clue as they gazed up into the heavens where Christ had ascended:

> … Men of Galilee, why do you stand looking into the sky? This Jesus, who has been taken up from you into heaven, will come in just the same way as you have watched Him go into heaven.[190]

Christ will descend similarly to the way He ascended (though obviously in reverse). And when He does, the **glory** believers have seen only with heavenly eyes amidst a decaying world will be confirmed in staggering intensity with their physical eyes.

Glory, *doxa* in Greek, is a word pregnant with meaning, but interestingly, it's derived from the word *dokeo*, which means "to think" or "to seem."[191] In biblical usage, it carries the idea of reputation or "weight," particularly in regard to God: "the glory of God is the worthiness of God, more particularly, the presence of God in the fullness of his attributes in some place or everywhere."[192]

The specific object of **glory** Paul writes about in this phrase is a bit confusing in the Greek, but the majority of scholars agree that **the appearing of the glory of our great God and Savior, Christ Jesus** refers solely to Jesus Christ, not God *and* Jesus Christ as two separate beings. Another way to read it would be "the appearing of our Savior Christ Jesus who reveals the glory of our great God."

God revealed His glory in many ways throughout the Old Testament. Perhaps the closest anyone ever got to witnessing it was Moses, as he led Israel through the wilderness after the exodus:

> Then Moses said, "I pray You, show me Your glory!" And He said, "I Myself will make all My goodness pass before you, and I

will proclaim the name of the Lord before you; and I will be gracious to whom I will be gracious, and will show compassion on whom I will show compassion." But He said, "You cannot see My face, for no man can see Me and live!" Then the Lord said, "Behold, there is a place by Me, and you shall stand there on the rock; and it will come about, while My glory is passing by, that I will put you in the cleft of the rock and cover you with My hand until I have passed by. Then I will take my hand away and you shall see My back, but My face shall not be seen" … It came about when Moses was coming down from Mount Sinai … that Moses did not know that the skin of his face shone because of his speaking with Him.[193]

This is amazing. Moses saw God's back—just the backside of His glory—and his face glowed … for a long time. His physical appearance literally changed just by seeing a glimpse of God's glory. The other Israelites didn't miss this intensity. They utterly freaked out when they saw him glowing—so much so that they made Moses wear a veil to cover his face.

God's glory is so extreme, human beings cannot even glimpse a full reveal of it without dying on the spot. It's terrifying, enthralling, mesmerizing, confounding, and heart-stopping. God is not some grandfatherly figure smoking a pipe in the sky, occasionally nodding or shaking His head at the behavior of His children. His presence is searing with such a potent culmination of goodness and truth, our fickle, feeble bodies cannot handle it. And we're not the only ones:

> … I saw the Lord sitting on a throne, lofty and exalted, with the train of His robe filling the temple. Seraphim stood above Him, each having six wings: with two he covered his face, and with two he covered his feet, and with two he flew. And one called out to another and said, "Holy, Holy, Holy, is the Lord of hosts, the whole earth is full of His glory." And the foundations of the

thresholds trembled at the voice of him who called out, while the temple was filling with smoke.[194]

These insanely awesome creatures, Seraphim, who exist in heaven and who have been around God for the entirety of their existence, can't even look at Him. Two of their wings cover their faces as they declare His glory and holiness. God cannot be contained; His glory cannot be fathomed.

As powerful as some Old Testament revelations of His glory were, the earth got an even greater reveal of God's glory with Jesus Christ. Jesus is the perfect manifestation of God's glory:

> … He is the radiance of His glory and the exact representation of His nature, and upholds all things by the word of His power …[195]

> And the Word became flesh, and dwelt among us, and we saw His glory, glory as of the only begotten from the Father, full of grace and truth.[196]

Jesus reveals God perfectly, yet we can look at Him and not die on the spot. He is 100 percent God, and Paul's description to Titus about His coming appearance "is perhaps the most un-ambiguous declaration in the New Testament of the deity of Jesus."[197] But He's also 100 percent man. He experienced human life in all its fullness, and as a result, "… we do not have a high priest who cannot sympathize with our weaknesses, but One who has been tempted in all things as we are, yet without sin.[198] Believers looked in eager anticipation of His coming once, and having received Him, now earnestly await His return.

WHO GAVE HIMSELF FOR US TO REDEEM US FROM EVERY LAWLESS DEED, AND TO PURIFY FOR HIMSELF A PEOPLE FOR HIS OWN POSSESSION, ZEALOUS FOR GOOD DEEDS.

Paul unequivocally attributes the full glory of God to Jesus Christ, the perfect demonstration of glory. Yet he also knows the Cretan Christians would probably benefit from further reminders about Jesus as motivation to carry out their godly lifestyles. Jesus' entire purpose for coming to earth was to fulfill the gospel—to make it possible for humanity to be reunited with God.

The moment sin entered the world through Adam and Eve, the world and everything in it was separated from God. Perfect fellowship became broken solitude. Ease of work became backbreaking effort. Manageable childbirth became unbearable pain. Companionship with animals became fearful distrust. Unhindered communication with God became restricted snippets. Sin broke everything—mankind's relationship with God, mankind's relationship with each other, and mankind's relationship with the world.

So depraved was the world, it couldn't even rescue itself. The only hope of salvation on one's own is to live the entirety of life without sin, which, of course, is entirely impossible. We are each born with a sin nature that immediately separates us from God, making salvation on our own merit an utterly hopeless pursuit.

Enter: Jesus.

Knowing we could never attain salvation on our own, He decided to pay the debt of our sin:

> When you were dead in your transgressions and the uncircumcision of your flesh, He made you alive together with Him, having forgiven us all our transgressions, having canceled out the certificate of debt consisting of decrees against us, which was hostile to us; and He has taken it out of the way, having nailed it to the cross.[199]

He fulfilled the demands of God's perfect justice while upholding His extension of perfect grace, and this happened by giving **Himself for us.** Jesus gave up everything so we could be restored to a right relationship with God:

> "… He existed in the form of God, did not regard equality with God a thing to be grasped, but emptied Himself, taking the form of a bond-servant, and being made in the likeness of men. Being found in appearance as a man, He humbled Himself by becoming obedient to the point of death, even death on a cross."[200]

Leaving heaven and all its perfect, glorious splendor, Jesus came to earth to die at the hand of people He came to save. He **gave Himself for us to redeem us from every lawless deed**, (including but certainly not limited to the horrifically egregious deed of crucifying Him). Again, thanks to Adam, we are each born into sin:

> Therefore, just as through one man sin entered into the world, and death through sin, and so death spread to all men, because all sinned.[201]

We, of course, match any inherent sin with intentional sin of our own, making us all guilty before God. In response to sin, God initially gave the world the Law (which began with the Ten Commandments given to Moses, interestingly at the same time he encountered the back of God's glory). The Law is God's standard of perfection required for anyone desiring to enter heaven. But since no one is capable of that, Jesus came:

> Do not think that I came to abolish the Law or the Prophets; I did not come to abolish but to fulfill.[202]

> For what the Law could not do, weak as it was through the flesh, God did: sending His own Son in the likeness of sinful flesh and

as an offering for sin, He condemned sin in the flesh, so that the requirement of the Law might be fulfilled in us, who do not walk according to the flesh but according to the Spirit.[203]

Our **lawless deeds** were paid for in full by Christ's lawful deeds, and Paul's choice of words is no accident. Cretans were well acquainted with lawless deeds; their lives, in fact, were consumed by them. Hence the contrast once again. What Cretans (like the rest of us) could never do on their own, Christ did on their behalf. Before they even knew they needed redemption, Christ accomplished it, in order **to purify for Himself a people for His own possession.**

To purify is to make clean, to cleanse from impurities, physical and spiritual alike. Clearly the emphasis Paul has in mind is a spiritual purity, though spiritual purity also involves an outward, physical manifestation. The imagery of purity laces itself throughout Scripture. In Psalm 51, David begs God to "create in me a clean [pure] heart, O God, and renew a steadfast spirit within me." Having written this psalm as a confession for his horrendous sins of adultery and murder; David sought purity in spirit as well as his life in general. Cretans were to do the same—yielding to the purification of their souls, which Christ offered through their redemption.

Christ was purifying **for Himself a people for His own possession.** The imagery of belonging to God—being His possession—is strong in both testaments. God chose Israel as His own early on:

> Now then, if you will indeed obey My voice and keep My covenant, then you shall be My own possession among all the peoples, for all the earth is Mine; and you shall be to Me a kingdom of priests and a holy nation ...[204]

> Who is a God like You, who pardons iniquity and passes over the rebellious act of the remnant of His possession? He does not

retain His anger forever, because He delights in unchanging love.[205]

"They will be Mine," says the Lord of hosts, "on the day that I prepare My own possession, and I will spare them as a man spares his own son who serves him."[206]

Despite Israel's many failures to live up to their calling as God's possession, He still cared for them and treated them with unrelenting grace, foreshadowing how He would one day relate to those who came to faith in Christ.

But you are a chosen race, a royal priesthood, a holy nation, a people for God's own possession, so that you may proclaim the excellencies of Him who has called you out of darkness into His marvelous light.[207]

Christians are chosen by God and belong to Him … and to each other. Those who are in Christ are never alone, "… for He Himself as said, 'I will never desert you, nor will I ever forsake you.'"[208] What a profound promise in an age in which connection can happen instantaneously, but people have never felt so alone. We belong to Him, and nothing in this world or the next can separate us from Him:

Who will separate us from the love of Christ? Will tribulation, or distress, or persecution, or famine, or nakedness, or peril, or sword? Just as it is written, "For Your sake we are being put to death all day long; we were considered as sheep to be slaughtered." But in all these things we overwhelmingly conquer through Him who loved us. For I am convinced that neither death, nor life, nor angels, nor principalities, nor things present, nor things to come, nor powers, nor height, nor depth, nor any other created thing, will be able to separate us from the love of God, which is in Christ Jesus our Lord.[209]

The organic response from those whom He calls His own is to be **zealous for good deeds.** In these four short words, Paul brings the entire passage (and the entire letter thus far) full circle. He begins the book by revealing His identity in Christ and mission in life, **for the faith of those chosen of God and the knowledge of the truth which is according to godliness, in the hope of eternal life.** He then moves on to helping Titus in his current assignment of establishing the Cretan church by providing a detailed list of life qualities to be present within anyone desiring the office of elder. The church needed solid leadership who lived out their faith, because of active theological threats within the community of believers. The men making these threats were leading others astray for their own gain. But Titus was to remain strong and teach church members (regardless of age, gender, or social status) how to embrace the gospel, not just by agreeing to it intellectually, but manifesting it in their lives. They were called to make the gospel beautiful and draw others to God by their actions and behaviors.

Paul knew it wasn't enough just to tell people to behave, so he then provides them with motivation to do so—**For the grace of God has appeared, bringing salvation to all men.** Living godly lives was but a response of Cretan believers to what Christ had already done for them (salvation, redemption, purification), and what He will do when He comes again. By living the most perfect example of faith possible, Christ redeems believers and inspires them to be **zealous for good deeds,** just as He was.

Christians aren't just to do good, they are to crave doing good. Obeying God and living out one's faith is not dreary and blind adherence to a list of rules. It's a compulsion, a burning desire and voracious yearning to be like Him, to give back to Him, motivated by all He has done for us. Jesus spoke two brief parables that reveal a proper response to those who have entered the kingdom of heaven:

> The kingdom of heaven is like a treasure hidden in the field, which a man found and hid again; and from joy over it he goes

and sells all that he has and buys that field. Again, the kingdom of heaven is like a merchant seeking fine pearls, and upon finding one pearl of great value, he went and sold all that he had and bought it.[210]

When Christians realize what they have in Christ, they give everything they have back to Him with eagerness and excitement. Just like the man who found a treasure in a field and sold everything to buy the field, Christians have found a treasure in Christ and give everything they are— give their lives—to pursue Him. Doing what pleases Him (good works) becomes a joy and privilege and, frankly, a small task in light of all He's done for them. His sacrifice and immeasurable grace becomes overwhelming motivation for His followers to do **good deeds** and to be thankful for the opportunity to do them.

THESE THINGS SPEAK AND EXHORT AND REPROVE WITH ALL AUTHORITY. LET NO ONE DISREGARD YOU.

All these truths Titus was to **speak and exhort and reprove with all authority,** letting **no one disregard** him. Paul has already told him to **speak the things which are fitting for sound doctrine** (2:1). Having now elaborated on that a bit, he reminds him once more to teach the truth **with all authority.**

These things refer to the entirety of chapter two in Titus—from the behavioral expectations of individual age/gender/status groupings to the theological doctrines of Christ that should motivate them to comply.[211] **Speak and exhort and reprove** have all been mentioned previously in this letter, referring to the different components an elder's leadership required of him. Elders (Titus included) were directed to **speak** the truth by verbally teaching or proclaiming it, to **exhort** or encourage passion for the gospel in Cretan believers' lives, and to **reprove** or correct congregants who erred.

All these actions were to be conducted **with all authority.** Paul specifically added **let no one disregard you,** for confirmation. Again, the church was new and immature at the time, especially on Crete. Titus had been trained by the Apostle Paul himself and had given his life to the advancement of the gospel and establishment of the church. But he still lacked resources. He didn't have a written copy of the New Testament to rely on, he didn't have an apostle physically present as a higher authority. And while he surely had some believers strong in faith surrounding him, he was the chosen apostolic delegate to the Cretan church.[212] That's a lot of worldly pressure for one man, and Satan would undoubtedly use it to cast doubt in Titus' mind.

Paul realizes the situation and reminds Titus who he is and that he must stand in full confidence in his authority, not just because he represents Paul to the Cretans, but because he represents Christ to them. Titus was to live as Christ's example to Crete in his teaching and his behavior. Since he took himself and his role seriously, others would as well.

Titus led the Cretan church with authority fueled by humility—he led as he first followed Christ. By speaking, exhorting, and reproving the gospel, he first had to know it; by being an authority, he had to live it. All of this, of course, was motivated by Christ. Though Titus' challenges were intense, they paled in comparison to the challenges Christ faced on his (and other believers') behalf. Thus, ministry was ultimately a joy; gospel-living a privilege.

GROUP STUDY

INTRODUCTION

> Motivation is perspective, letting the future drive the present.

Motivation is the reason behind everything we say, think, and do. Without it, goals are unrealized, projects are left undone, and adrenaline is absent, even in the most menial of tasks.

- What are some common motivations in our culture?

- What has motivated you to accomplish goals in the past?

THE WORD

Every pursuit is driven by motivation, but not every motive is good or right. Losing weight to be healthy is good; losing weight to be accepted or approved by society, not so good. Excelling at work to be an example of responsibility and to provide for family is good; excelling at work to show off or seek a better self-image, not so good.

Paul knows that while obeying God is a good pursuit, the motivation for doing so is just as important as the act itself. So he gives Titus and the Cretan believers a brief overview of the theology that should motivate every good deed and godly behavior in their lives:

> For the grace of God has appeared, bringing salvation to all men, instructing us to deny ungodliness and worldly desires and to live sensibly, righteously and godly in the present age, looking for the blessed hope and the appearing of the glory of our great God and Savior, Christ Jesus, who gave Himself for us to redeem us from

every lawless deed, and purify for Himself a people for His own possession, zealous for good deeds. (Titus 2:11-15)

- What has appeared?

    - What is that, exactly?

    - What did it bring?

        - What does that entail?

    - Who did He bring it to?

- What does the gospel instruct believers to do?

    To deny _____ and _____ _____

    to live _____, _____ and _____

    in this present age.

- What's significant about this two-part process, both "to deny …" and then "to live …"?

- As believers follow those instructions, what are they to look for?

    - What, if anything, do you know about that event?

    - What role does this event play in the cosmic unfolding of the gospel?

- What has Christ Jesus done for believers?

    - _____

    - _____

    - _____

- How does Christ's sacrifice impact a believer's motivation to do good?

APPLY

Righteous living is a means, not an end. Anyone can appear upright in behavior, but only those motivated by Christ will *be* upright and *yearn* to do right because of what Christ has done for them.

"Woe to you, scribes and Pharisees, hypocrites! For you are like whitewashed tombs which on the outside appear beautiful, but inside they are full of dead men's bones and all uncleanness. So you, too, outwardly appear righteous to men, but inwardly you are full of hypocrisy and lawlessness."
Jesus, Matthew 23:27-28

"Let us rejoice and be glad and give the glory to Him, for the marriage of the Lamb has come and His bride has made herself ready."
The Great Heavenly Multitude, Revelation 19:7

As Christians, we aren't just to live well. Rather, we have a burning *desire* to live well because of the overwhelming, unfathomable, inexhaustible mercies we have received (and will continue receiving) in Christ. We don't earn or keep salvation by works; good works are a response of gratitude for the salvation we have already received and will experience entirely one day in heaven. But as we eagerly wait for that day, we can live out our profound thankfulness now by pleasing Him with the lives He died to save.

- In what ways are your motivations for godly living perhaps not what they should be?

- What aspects of Christ's sacrifice do you find particularly motivating?

- What are some practical ways you can lean on them this week as you strive to live out your faith?

WEEK FIVE
TITUS 3:1-8

PERSONAL BIBLE STUDY QUESTIONS

1. Who are Cretan Christians supposed to be subject to? (3:1)

2. What are they supposed to be ready for? (3:1)

3. How should they relate to each other and all people in general? (3:2)

   a)

   b)

   c)

   d)

4. What characterized believers before they came to Christ? (3:3)

   a)

   b)

   c)

   d)

e)

f)

5. What appeared in the midst of their sin? (3:4)

    a)

    b)

6. On what basis did God *not* save us? (3:5)

7. What role does the Holy Spirit play in salvation? (3:5)

8. What are we made into, "according to the hope of eternal life"? (3:7)

9. What is good and profitable for men? (3:8)

COMMENTARY

> Remind them to be subject to rulers, to authorities, to be obedient, to be ready for every good deed, to malign no one, to be peaceable, gentle, showing every consideration for all men. For we also once were foolish ourselves, disobedient, deceived, enslaved to various lusts and pleasures, spending our life in malice and envy, hateful, hating one another. But when the kindness of God our Savior and His love for mankind appeared, He saved us, not on the basis of deeds which we have done in righteousness, but according to His mercy, by the washing of regeneration and renewing by the Holy Spirit, whom He poured out upon us richly through Jesus Christ our Savior, so that being justified by His grace we would be made heirs according to the hope of eternal life. This is a trustworthy statement; and concerning these things I want you to speak confidently, so that those who have believed God will be careful to engage in good deeds. These things are good and profitable for men.
>
> Titus 3:1-8

Memory is a powerful tool that brings either life or death, depending on how we use it. Life, in that it can help us remember truth and avoid past mistakes (either we or others have made), allowing us to thrive and grow. Death, in that it can keep us enslaved to the past, unable to move beyond certain experiences or relationships that bind us.

Paul has instructed Titus (and Cretan believers by direct extension) how Christians are to live out their faith as motivated by the gospel of Jesus Christ. But motivation, like truth in general, needs to be recalled in order to be effective. Righteous living isn't easy, especially in a society as debased as Crete's was at the time. Barbs of immorality constantly attacked any fortress of truth Cretan Christians managed to construct around their hearts and minds.

Implementing an entirely different worldview into one's life is difficult, even without constant attack, because we are used to our old lives and ways of doing things. Consider what happens when the electricity goes out during a storm. We know the electricity is out, but we still reach for light switches immediately upon entering a room. Why? Because we're used to it. It's an automatic response, ingrained in our minds over years and years of repetitive behavior. If environmental habits are hard to break, we shouldn't expect spiritual ones to be easy to part with either.

Paul realizes Cretan Christians need all the help they can get to practice the truth of the gospel in their daily lives, and he provides them with yet another tool to do so. The next directive he gives Titus, then, is to help Cretans remember the truth they've been taught, how deplorable their lives were prior to Christ, and how Christ saved them so they could experience eternal life.

REMIND THEM TO BE SUBJECT TO RULERS, TO AUTHORITIES, TO BE OBEDIENT, TO BE READY FOR EVERY GOOD DEED.

In the majority of Christian circles, believers need to be reminded of truth a whole lot more than they need to be taught it. We far too easily forget what once enthralled us, far too easily neglect what we once cherished, and are far too easily satisfied with the grime of this world, when God offers riches immeasurable. C.S. Lewis, in his sermon "The Weight of Glory," describes it beautifully:

> It would seem that our Lord finds our desires not too strong, but too weak. We are half-hearted creatures, fooling about with drink and sex and ambition when infinite joy is offered us, like an ignorant child who wants to go on making mud pies in a slum because he cannot imagine what is meant by the offer of a holiday at the sea. We are far too easily pleased.

When we meet Christ, we stand in awe. How can we not? He's irresistible! But before long, we fall back into the same old habits, the same old way of thinking, and the same old destructive relationships. We forget and neglect the brilliant majesty of our Creator and choose "mud pies in a slum" instead, because they're comfortable. They're what we're used to. We don't think we've been living that badly, surely not as bad as some, so we're content keeping Jesus and our get-out-of-hell-free card on a dusty shelf in our minds.

This isn't new. Israel stands infamous in their penchant for forgetting God, His truth, and all He had done for them:

> The sons of Israel did what was evil in the sight of the Lord, and forgot the Lord their God and served the Baals and the Asheroth.[213]

> They forgot His deeds and His miracles that He had shown them.[214]

> They quickly forgot His works; they did not wait for His counsel.[215]

> Thus the sons of Israel did not remember the Lord their God, who had delivered them from the hands of all their enemies on every side.[216]

Despite committing themselves to God and having witnessed world-changing miracles numerous times, Israel forgot Him. They prioritized the temporary over the eternal, the physical over the supernatural, and the comfortable over the life-transforming. They needed to be reminded of God's truth—what He had done for them, what He was doing for them, and what He would do for them—over and over and over again.

Remember the days of old, consider the years of all generations. Ask your father, and he will inform you, your elders, and they will tell you.[217]

Remember His wonderful deeds which He has done, His marvels and the judgments from His mouth.[218]

Remember His covenant forever, the word which He commanded to a thousand generations.[219]

Remember the former things long past, for I am God, and there is no other; I am God, and there is no one like Me.[220]

We need the same thing. Just like Israel, we need to be reminded of His truth. We need to remember what He's done, what He is doing, and what He will do as His gospel advances throughout the world. The gospel absolutely must stay at the forefront of our minds if we are to have any chance of living it out.

That's why Paul tells Titus to **remind them** (the Cretan believers). In the Greek, it actually reads "keep reminding them" of the truth they are to live out amidst a dark and pagan culture.[221] Specifically, they are to be reminded **to be subject to rulers, to authorities.**

Sinful, human nature despises authority. We don't have to teach our children to argue, disobey, or throw tantrums when we say no. Defiant attitudes stand at the core of our fallen genetic code and display themselves even before we can walk. Cretans owned this inherent partiality for rebellion and put it to practice often with "insurrections, murders and internecine wars."[222] To **be subject to rulers, to authorities,** then, was an instruction of great humility for Cretan believers. Having been bred in a society who prided themselves on insubordination, putting on a gospel perspective of service and compliance as unto the Lord tested their faith and would've raised a few eyebrows. Of course, drawing positive attention to themselves was a goal, a way to draw others closer to Christ by the way they lived.

Due to great political unrest in that day, the subject of authority (and submission to it) is familiar throughout the New Testament. God makes it clear that all authority ultimately comes from Him:

> Every person is to be in subjection to the governing authorities. For there is no authority except from God, and those which exist are established by God.[223]

> For by Him all things were created, both in the heavens and on earth, visible and invisible, whether thrones or dominions or rulers or authorities—all things have been created through Him and for Him.[224]

God created leadership to reflect Himself and to establish order in creation. When we are **subject to rulers, to authorities**, we subject ourselves to God and honor the leadership He placed in our lives.

Paul also knows that a posture of submissiveness to government authority translates naturally to submissiveness to spiritual authority. And "ministers of the gospel will have no authority if they do not teach the people of God to respect authority."[225] Cretans' issues with compliance most likely seeped into church authority, of which Titus stood at the forefront. Paul wanted to create an environment of humility and respect for authority among the Cretan church, which of course begins in their posture toward God, but then filters down to government and spiritual authorities as well. After having been taught this posture, they needed to be reminded often, as the Holy Spirit helped root it in their lives.

His specific instruction to Titus here speaks of authority in general, of rulers who, although maybe not ideal, should still receive respect and honor. Believers were to be peaceable, responsible, law-abiding citizens who behaved in a way that shed light on Christ and inspired others to draw near to Him.

Jesus had much to say on the matter of government, especially since Jews expected the Messiah to overthrow the Romans and make Jews the rulers. Jews hated being under Roman authority and assumed the Savior would save them politically. When it became clear that Jesus had no intention of overthrowing governments, the Jewish leaders despised and plotted against Him, using the heated subject of government adherence as ammunition:

> Then the Pharisees went and plotted together how they might trap Him in what He said. And they sent their disciples to Him, along with the Herodians, saying, "Teacher, we know that You are truthful and teach the way of God in truth, and defer to no one; for You are not partial to any. Tell us then, what do You think? Is it lawful to give a poll-tax to Caesar, or not?" But Jesus perceived their malice, and said, "Why are you testing Me, you hypocrites? Show Me the coin used for the poll-tax." And they brought Him a denarius. And He said to them, "Whose likeness and inscription is this?" They said to Him, "Caesar's." Then He said to them, "Then render to Caesar the things that are Caesar's; and to God the things that are God's." And hearing this, they were amazed, and leaving Him, they went away.[226]

The brilliance of Jesus' response is not surprising (He is God, after all), and confirms God's perspective of government: He established it, allows it, and is in ultimate control of it. Therefore, mankind is to subject themselves to it. Caesar was hardly a righteous man, but Jesus respected his authority and submitted Himself to it as an example for us to follow.

Fortunately, most government structures in the world today make it relatively easy for us to submit. While they may permit more than what is morally acceptable (like abortion), they don't demand it. But sometimes, in some countries, earthly authority stands blatantly against God, and demands we do so as well. Again, this is not what Paul has in mind as he's writing to Titus.

It's an exception to be reasonably explored.

Herod, a king whom God allowed to stand in leadership, detested Christians and wanted them gone. So he "… had James the brother of John put to death with a sword."[227] Was this righteous? Should believers of that day have submitted to him? Herod stood under God's authority, although he didn't realize it, and grossly abused his God-given authority. But yes, James stood in subjection to Herod and, as a citizen, was expected to behave respectfully. But when he had to choose between his faith and obedience to Herod, he chose correctly to stand firm in the gospel and pay for it with his life.

If the law demands Christians cease to proclaim the gospel or live out their faith, the time has come to *respectfully* disagree. We're not to act rashly, but rather should take every reasonable action necessary to stand up for what's right in a way that honors the God we're doing it for.

For today's Americans, this isn't nearly as dire as it sometimes was back then. While our government is hardly godly, it also doesn't typically (if ever) force us to do anything contrary to our beliefs. It does occasionally produce laws that stand contrary to the gospel, and when that happens, we should take reasonable, responsible, appropriate civil action against it. In other words, any and all protests should be peaceable, and the manner in which they are conducted should uphold other laws. We are in subjection to the governing authorities God has placed over us, and the way we conduct ourselves as citizens goes a long way toward revealing Christ to the world around us.

In the majority of instances, we are to respond to authority as Cretan Christians did—**to be obedient.** Paul still has the state and governing authorities in mind with this edict of obedience. The concept of being **subject** is similar to obedience of Christians to their current governing system. This is not blind, rote, or mechanical conformity conducted out of fear, duty, or obligation. Rather, Christians are to be **sensible** and take "every thought captive to the obedience of Christ" first, [228] for that is where our identity, purpose, and eternal security lie.

But when government doesn't directly contradict God and attempt to force believers into doing what's immoral (the majority of governments don't), Christ-believing citizens are **to be obedient.** This includes but isn't limited to all traffic laws, honest taxes, drug and alcohol laws, proper domestic relations, not stealing, etc. Christians are not to exceed the speed limit just as they are not to commit murder. We aren't above the government God has placed over us. Just because we don't like a law or don't agree with it (direct contradiction with God notwithstanding), that doesn't mean we can exempt ourselves from total and peaceable compliance. Being **subject** means we willingly **obey** the laws of our government in all our actions.

Willing obedience to governing authority includes being **ready for every good deed,** which means going above and beyond base obligations to "an active, positive involvement in society."[229] Jesus advocated this in the Sermon on the Mount when He said, "Whoever forces you to go one mile, go with him two."[230] Under Roman rule, soldiers and other authorities transported goods across the land frequently. Along the way, it was the government's right "to commandeer a man at any place and they would make him carry the baggage from that stage to the next."[231] These commandeered men weren't to be resentful for the interruption in their day, nor were they to complain, be angry, or try to get out of it. Rather, they were to comply willingly. Not only that, they were to do so with such a pleasing attitude that they performed double the amount of the demanded task. In other words, they were to **be ready for every good deed**, actively looking for ways to serve and display their love for Christ by the way they adhered to the governing laws of their day.

Cretan Christians were to abide by the same perspective, which fought against every natural political impulse they'd been taught growing up. But therein lies the beauty. In pleasantly complying with a government's demands in a culture bent on fighting them, they stood out. Standing out in a positive way provides a great opportunity to share the gospel. When people wonder why someone would display such an attitude, they ask about it, and the believer has a chance to share the reason—because Christ did so much more for them, and He compels them to do the same for others.

TO MALIGN NO ONE, TO BE PEACEABLE, GENTLE, SHOWING EVERY CONSIDERATION FOR ALL MEN.

With others in mind, Paul makes a slight shift from governmental authorities to public behavior in general. While Cretan believers needed to be reminded to submit to ruling powers, they also had to remember **to malign no one, to be peaceable, gentle, showing consideration for all men.** People watched the church and the way believers acted in public and how they reflected God, for better or worse.

To malign is to speak evil or injuriously toward another individual.[232] Interestingly, this is the same word, *blasphemeo*, used back in chapter two, verse five when younger women are instructed "to be sensible, pure, workers at home, kind, being subject to their own husbands, so that the word of God will not be *dishonored"* (maligned, *blasphemeo).* Christians can **malign** the Word of God by not fulfilling their roles appropriately just as they can **malign** each other in the way they speak.

Immediate contexts carry the most weight in determining the specific meanings of words. Consider the word "love." In English, love encompasses a broad spectrum of nuances. We love our spouses, we love pizza, we love our jobs, we love our children, we love the way a new blouse fits, we love a new song. Love means a lot of things, depending on its context. The same is true for words in any language, including the original Greek the New Testament was written in.

Thus, *blasphemeo* can mean one of several things, depending on its context. In the context of Paul later in his letter to Titus, the general definition of speaking evil or slandering against other individuals is preferred, whereas previously when discussing the relationship between behavior and the Word of God, a heavier definition of blasphemy is appropriate.[233] Cretan Christians were to avoid harsh words to each other, regardless of circumstance.

Our words matter, and *how* we speak to each other is just as important as *what* we speak. James warns of the power of the tongue:

> Now if we put the bits into the horses' mouths so that they will obey us, we direct their entire body as well. Look at the ships also, though they are so great and are driven by strong winds, are still directed by a very small rudder wherever the inclination of the pilot desires. So also the tongue is a small part of the body, and yet it boasts of great things. See how great a forest is set aflame by such a small fire![234]

The tongue is small, yet mighty. It holds the power to build up or destroy. Even the smallest, simplest words spoken in malice can cause a ripple effect of devastation, harming an entire body of believers. Christians are to control their tongues and open their mouths only to speak truth to one another in a manner becoming of Christ:

> ... Speaking the truth in love, we are to grow up in all aspects into Him who is the head, even Christ, from whom the whole

body, being fitted and held together by what every joint supplies, according to the proper working of each individual part, causes the growth of the body for the building up of itself in love ... therefore, laying aside falsehood, speak truth each one of you with his neighbor, for we are members of one another.[235]

Remembering that we belong to one another and are in the same family of Christ will help us speak kindly to each other, in love and in truth. When we speak with gentleness, we build each other up and, by default, build up the entire body of Christ.

Speaking the truth in love lays a foundation of peace in our relationships, both with each other and the world around us. Titus was to remind Cretans **to be peaceable,** which literally means "not fighting."[236] Being peaceable obviously includes refraining from physical blows with one another, but it more potently means refraining from altercations of any kind and instead intentionally pursuing goodwill and unity.

As with every other behavior, being **peaceable** signifies the status of one's heart with God. If we are at peace with God, it's much easier to be at peace with one another. When we're not, quarreling becomes a constant temptation:

> What is the source of quarrels and conflicts among you? Is not the source your pleasures that wage war in your members? You lust and do not have; so you commit murder. You are envious and cannot obtain; so you fight and quarrel ... you adulteresses, do you not know that friendship with the world is hostility toward God? Therefore whoever wishes to be a friend of the world makes himself an enemy of God.[237]

When our souls aren't at peace, our relationships aren't either. St. Augustine said, "You have made us for yourself, O Lord, and our heart is restless until it rests in you."[238] When we desire anything but God or when we put anything in God's place in our lives and hearts, we become restless and take it out on those around us. That's not how it's supposed to be. God desires all people to be at peace with Him and to then be at peace with one another. This is how He originally created the world, and that's how it will be again when we meet Him face to face. Until then, we strive to make peace a reality in our lives, just as Cretan Christians did.

Being **peaceable** in our relationships often requires us to be **gentle, showing every consideration for all men.** The two words used here (**gentle** and **consideration**) overlap a bit in the original Greek. In fact, the Greek word for **consideration,** *praytes,* is translated "gentle" throughout the New Testament. But while they are similar, they are distinct.

Gentleness, *epieikes,* in this instance means considerate, reasonable, forbearing, courteous, or conciliatory.[239] Cretan Christians were to "be willing to defer to others, although it may require them to relinquish some of their own rights."[240] They must be flexible, not so intent on being right or upholding rules that they miss out on an opportunity for good and to show grace to someone else. Aristotle described this word as "the ability 'to consider not only the letter of the law, but also the mind and intention of the legislator.' Someone who is *epieikes* is always ready to avoid the injustice which often lies in being strictly just."[241] To be **gentle,** then, is to be reasonable and to put the good of others first, opting for grace instead of strict adherence to the rules.

Consider an employer/employee relationship as an example. An employee, John, is typically exceptional at work, fulfilling his duties promptly and with humility and excellence. One day John arrives at work late, breaking the one rule his employer, Bruce, is particularly uptight about. When John arrives ten minutes past starting time, Bruce would technically have been justified in immediately attacking him with condemnation and judgment. Instead, Bruce opts to be **gentle.** He takes John's past and reputation into consideration, putting his good first, and asks how his morning has been. John quickly confesses his horrendous morning and details the extensive list of circumstantial events that led him to be tardy, profusely apologizing along the way. Because Bruce opted for gentleness instead of harshness (even though it may have been his right as employer), John's morning turned around at work. Because he received gentleness, he was eager to do his work well, and so were any others who heard about the situation. Gentleness looked beyond the circumstance to the benefit of the individual. That's how Cretan Christians were to relate to those around them.

Wrapping up this short list that began with instructions for believers' posture toward governmental authority and then shifted to general public behavior, Paul tells Titus to remind believers to show **every consideration for all men.** This phrase translates as "to show true humility to all men," the Greek word, *prauteta,* meaning gentleness and meekness.[242] This word is difficult to express in English, because it seems to communicate weakness or timidity, which isn't true at all. Rather, "it must be clearly understood … that the meekness manifested by the Lord and commended to the believer is the fruit of power. The common assumption is that when a man is meek, it is because he cannot help himself; but the Lord was 'meek' because he had the infinite resources of God at His command," and yet controlled how He manifested them.[243]

The same root of this word is used to describe Christ (translated as "gentle"):

> Come to Me, all who are weary and heavy-laden, and I will give you rest. Take My yoke upon you and learn from Me, for I am gentle and humble in heart, and you will find rest for your souls.[244]

> Say to the daughter of Zion, "Behold your King is coming to you, gentle, and mounted on a donkey …"[245]

... Paul, myself urge you by the meekness and gentleness of Christ...[246]

Since Christ is our motivation for everything and served as the perfect example, which we follow, it's only logical that we should manifest similar traits. Further, gentleness (or **showing consideration**) is a fruit of the Spirit:

> But the fruit of the Spirit is love, joy, peace, patience, kindness, goodness, faithfulness, gentleness, self-control, against such things there is no law.[247]

Thus, if we have been saved by Christ and are sealed with His Holy Spirit, who actively works in and through our lives to make us more like our Savior, then we are to exhibit Jesus' very character. Having the power of the Holy Spirit means we must act with **consideration for all men,** harnessing the strength given us and using it to build others up as Christ did.

Paul follows his own advice by reminding believers to show **every consideration for all men in** several other places throughout the New Testament (again, translated as gentleness). Believers are to be restored with gentleness after a trespass,[248] to walk in a manner worthy of their calling with all gentleness,[249] to put on a heart of gentleness as those who have been chosen by God,[250] and to pursue gentleness.[251] Cretan Christians, under Titus' leadership and against an environment of hostility and disrespect, should stand out by **showing consideration for all men,** being reasonable, considerate, and courteous in all their relationships, public and private.

FOR WE ALSO ONCE WERE FOOLISH OURSELVES, DISOBEDIENT, DECEIVED, ENSLAVED TO VARIOUS LUSTS AND PLEASURES, SPENDING OUR LIFE IN MALICE AND ENVY, HATEFUL, HATING ONE ANOTHER.

Just as Cretan Christians needed to be reminded to let their behavior toward authorities and each other reflect Christ, they also needed to remember where they came from. We all do. Again, memory is a powerful tool that can be used for death or life, for bad or good. When we use it to remember where we came from and who we were prior to Christ, we more fully embrace the eternal lives we have in Him. When awareness of our past depravity becomes fresh in our minds, its realness and intensity can momentarily overwhelm us. But only for a brief moment. Then we're reminded of Christ and His power in salvation, which exposed and redeemed even the deepest, most hidden crevices of sin in our souls. We've experienced both; we need to remember both. The more acutely we feel the weight of our debasement before Christ, the more liberated we feel in glorious elation, having received Him.

Paul wants Titus to remind the Cretan Christians of their former lives, prior to Christ. But for two reasons, they should never look at the posture they came from in arrogance or loftiness. First, they did nothing to take themselves out of it. Second, such an attitude would automatically translate to others who were currently in that position, making grace and love toward them difficult to exercise. The purpose of this memory, then, is to recognize the weight and power of sin so they could then know the *greater* weight and power of Christ and the gospel that freed them from that sin.

For we also once were foolish ourselves. The Cretan culture was easily and accurately described as **foolish.** They pursued selfish impulses without regard to moral or practical consequences, were thoughtless in their conduct, and prioritized temporary pleasures over long-term profit. While Paul certainly includes the Cretan society in this text, by using the term **we** (Paul, Titus, Christians in general), he refers more specifically to the general foolishness of humanity before Christ—the dark state of their consuming sin.

Foolish, *anoetos* in Greek, carries with it a sense of being thoughtless,[252] lacking sense and sensibility in both mental and moral capacities.[253] In a spiritual sense, being **foolish** "denotes spiritual obtuseness or ignorance specifically of God."[254] Before salvation, we are each blind when it comes to God and life in Him. Whether we know absolutely nothing about Him or we hold a degree in theology, before we experience the gospel, we are outsiders. We simply don't get it because we don't know Him.

In my college years, I had an exceedingly bright friend. We spent hours talking our way around ideas, philosophies, and worldviews. Our conversations were deep, with quite a bit of sarcastic wit thrown about to keep the mood light, since he was not a believer and I was. Probably for no other reason than to fuel our conversations, he took a Bible course that was taught from the standpoint of literature—the Bible as a literary masterpiece or some such title. As you can imagine, he read the Bible a lot in that class, studied it, and even wrote papers about it. In every conversation we had during that time, he could tell me the superficial meaning of a passage, but he missed its link to the gospel (and thus, to God) completely. And there was nothing I could do (trust me, I spewed out many a word) to make him get it. The Holy Spirit didn't reside in him. He was blind to the depth and wisdom and glory and treasure that is God's Word. We parted ways, and while I don't know where he is today, I pray that his eyes have since been enlightened—that God has drawn him near so he is no longer **foolish** in his gospel understanding.

That's the kind of foolishness Paul is talking about here. While it definitely can include being stupid, it's better understood in the context of lacking a Spirit-given understanding of the gospel.

> For the word of the cross is foolishness to those who are perishing, but to us who are being saved it is the power of God. For it is written, "I will destroy the wisdom of the wise, and the cleverness of the clever I will set aside." Where is the wise man?

Where is the scribe? Where is the debater of this age? Has not God made foolish the wisdom of the world? For since in the wisdom of God the world through its wisdom did not come to know God, God was well-pleased through the foolishness of the message preached to save those who believe … For consider your calling, brethren, that there were not many wise according to the flesh, not many mighty, not many noble; but God has chosen the foolish things of the world to shame the wise, and God has chosen the weak things of the world to shame the things which are strong.[255]

If we don't have the Holy Spirit enlightening our minds with truth, we are inevitably **disobedient** to mandates derived from said truth. **Disobedient** (*apeithes*) means "rebellious against God" more than rebellious against authoritative institutions of man.[256] Paul's already used this word to describe false teachers earlier in this letter, by saying, "they profess to know God, but by their deeds they deny Him, being detestable and **disobedient** and worthless for any good deed."[257] Even the most self-ascribed pious individuals are blatant rebels apart from Christ. As lost souls, we are all **foolish** and **disobedient**—incapable of doing anything good because our hearts are hopelessly wayward:

The heart is more deceitful than all else and is desperately sick; who can understand it? I, the Lord, search the heart, I test the mind, even to give to each man according to his ways, according to the results of his deeds.[258]

Our hearts are dead in sin and cannot be trusted. Some of the worst advice ever is to "follow your heart." Before Christ, our hearts are vile and will always lead us astray in disobedience. After Christ, there are certainly times when our hearts are in sync with God, but we are still never to let them lead. We follow Christ, period. We let truth reign and keep our emotions on the side as an accessory. Our emotions are fickle, fleeting, and ever-changing; they make terrible guides and often lead straight to disobedience. If ever our emotions conflict with our knowledge of the truth, we're to kick emotion aside and cling to what we know pleases God.

Some may argue, "Surely we can't be held responsible for our foolishness and disobedience before Christ. We didn't know any better!" Despite our minds being dark and our hearts being sick, neither foolishness nor disobedience is excused. Neither lets you off the hook when you meet Jesus face to face one day:

> For the wrath of God is revealed from heaven against all ungodliness and unrighteousness of men who suppress the truth in unrighteousness, because that which is known about God is evident within them; for God made it evident to them. For since the creation of the world His invisible attributes, His eternal power and divine nature, have been clearly seen, being understood through what has been made, so that they are without excuse.[259]

We are without excuse. God has made His existence obvious in creation around us (despite evolutionary claims otherwise), and has given us a moral compass as well. We intuitively know it's wrong to murder, rape, steal, lie; you don't have to know Jesus personally to be convinced of that. God's given us so much evidence of His existence that everyone is without excuse. We are each **foolish** and **disobedient** before Christ, lost without any hope of being found on our own.

As if that wasn't bad enough, we were also **deceived.** Without God, we have no hope of encountering gospel truth. Unfortunately, there are those within the realm of faith who actively try to lead people astray as well (like the Jewish false teachers from earlier).

Truth is something we all strive for or think we have attained (even by denying its existence), but in reality, apart from God we believe nothing but a huge lie from the devil himself. Satan is good at what he does, sprinkling just enough truth in his lies that they seem reasonable and sure. His trickery is real, and its consequences are eternally dire.

Consider Eve, deceived:

> Now the serpent was more crafty than any beast of the field which the Lord God had made. And he said to the woman, "Indeed, has God said, 'You shall not eat from any tree of the garden'?" The woman said to the serpent, "From the fruit of the trees of the garden we may eat; but from the fruit of the tree which is in the middle of the garden, God has said, 'You shall not eat from it or touch it, or you will die.'" The serpent said to the woman, "You surely will not die! For God knows that in the day you eat from it your eyes will be opened, and you will be like God, knowing good and evil." When the woman saw that the tree was good for food, and that it was a delight to the eyes, and that the tree was desirable to make one wise, she took from its fruit and ate; and she gave also to her husband with her, and he ate. Then the eyes of both of them were opened...[260]

Satan begins his strategy by questioning God's Word. His initial question contains a whole lot of truth (did God say you can't eat from any tree?) with one glaring exception, which Eve catches and proceeds to overcorrect. (She said they could eat from all but one, but that one they couldn't eat or touch. But God never told them not to touch it). Then Satan directly contradicts God by telling Eve she wouldn't really die if she ate it, that God knows eating it will make her like Him, and He doesn't want that. Lies, lies, lies ... all grounded in warped, but real, truth. Eve is now confused and takes a look at the fruit she probably never gave a second glance before. All of a sudden, it's attractive and tempting and ... she eats. She then shares some with Adam, who was standing right next to her the entire time. (Way to lead, Adam). They sin for the first time in creation's history and contaminate every single soul who would ever come into existence after them.

They bear the blame, though Satan's not entirely exempt. Nor has he been exempt in the countless deceptions he's introduced to the world since. But not all fall prey to his lies.

Consider Jesus' response to the devil's temptation:

> Then Jesus was led up by the Spirit into the wilderness to be tempted by the devil. And after He had fasted forty days and forty nights, He then became hungry. And the tempter came and said to Him, "If You are the Son of God, command that these stones become bread." But He answered and said, "It is written, 'Man shall not live on bread alone, but on every word that proceeds out of the mouth of God.'" Then the devil took Him into the holy city and had Him stand on the pinnacle of the temple, and said to Him, "If You are the Son of God, throw Yourself down; for it is written, 'He will command His angels concerning You'; and 'On their hands they will bear You up, so that You will not strike Your foot against a stone.'" Jesus said to him, "On the other hand, it is written, 'You shall not put the Lord your God to the test.'" Again, the devil took Him to a very high mountain and showed Him all the kingdoms of the world and their glory; and he said to Him, "All these things I will give You, if You fall down and worship me." Then Jesus said to him, "Go, Satan! For it is written, 'You shall worship the Lord your God, and serve Him only.'" Then the devil left Him; and behold, angels came and began to minister to Him.[261]

Satan knows God's Word better than most church leaders do. He even tried to use it against Jesus Christ Himself! But Jesus, of course, knows it too and used it *in its proper context* to ward off Satan's temptations and, ultimately, to send him away.

Before Christ, we are all grossly deceived, and Satan would like nothing more than to keep us that way if he's already lost the battle of our souls. When we come to Christ, our eyes are opened and He reveals His truth to us, breaking the bond of deception that previously clouded our minds. But having the Holy Spirit does not mean we automatically interpret Scripture correctly every single time. We, like Jesus, need to exercise proper hermeneutics when interpreting and applying the Bible to our lives; otherwise, we will end up like Eve and so many after her, who fall prey to the devil's lies even after salvation.

Before Christ, we were **foolish, disobedient, deceived,** and **enslaved to various lusts and pleasures.** Again we come to the topic of slavery. But slavery to sin (specifically, the **various lusts and pleasures** we pursued prior to Christ) more closely resembles the bondage of addicts to their vice than the willing yielding of oneself to another out of love. Slavery to sin before salvation offers no hope of freedom. It's oppressive, cruel, soul-wrenching, depressing, and utterly hopeless without the divine intervention of God Himself.

Various lusts and pleasures may initially sound tempting (there's a reason Las Vegas is so popular), but the kind of pleasure the world offers is fleeting, deceptive, and shallow. It doesn't last. It leaves us empty, and the only way we continue experiencing its thrill is by going deeper and deeper into it. Once we've reached a certain point, our willing participation becomes a rabid addiction that's never satisfied. That's sin. That's the kind of slavery our souls experience before we come to Christ.

Another dreadful aspect of a soul's life prior to salvation is the fact that we were **spending our life in malice and envy.** Both of these describe internal iniquities, symptoms of hearts far from God. **Malice,** or *kakia* in Greek, "depicts a life turned toward evil."[262] It's the only posture our lives could take, because the only alternative would be to turn toward God, and we've already established that's impossible without Him first instilling faith into our hearts and drawing us near to Him. All we're capable of prior to Christ is evil, as the Cretan culture showed us. Even our "good" deeds are tainted with sin and bear no eternal value.

Envy is straightforward. It's jealousy of what you don't have but see in others. This is a particularly nasty sin. Not only does it cause other sins, like bitterness, anger, and complaining, but it also destroys relationships. Envy and malice "are very ugly twins … malice is wishing people evil, while envy is resenting and coveting their good."[263] Both eat up the souls of those who harness them, both are difficult to get rid of, and both thoroughly wreck relationships.

Such internal evil can't help but seep out, resulting in lives that are **hateful, hating one another.** If anything was the direct opposite of God, it's hate. While He does hate sin, the overwhelming consistent posture of God toward humanity is love. "Greater love has no one than this, that one lay down his life for his friends … We know love by this, that He laid down His life for us."[264] Those who hate are not of God, for believers are known by their love for one another.[265] Thus, our lives prior to Christ were marked by hate. We didn't know what real love was and definitely were not able to experience it because, as with good deeds, everything was tainted with sin and selfish motivations.

The word **hateful**, here, *stygetos*, is used only once in this syntax in the entire New Testament. It's a passive term that can also be translated as "being hated."[266] In essence, then, our former lives were marked by being hated and then **hating one another**. No one in their right mind enjoys being hated; quite the opposite. We crave attention, approval, and love. But since we didn't know what real love was or where it came from, we pursued it in all the wrong places and in all the wrong ways. When it falls through, as it always does, we're left angry, disappointed, miserable, alone, and **hating one another**—"totally absorbed with the destruction of others to preserve oneself."[267]

Hating one another involves a level of selfishness known only by those who've never experienced otherwise. Before Christ, our souls are restless, and the more failures we endure to pacify our internal, eternal longing, the more bitter and dejected we become. Then the blaming begins. We start blaming other people when they don't fill the God-sized hole in our hearts. If we idolize relationships, we blame and even hate our exes for not fulfilling us and meeting all our expectations. If we idolize careers, we blame others for any setbacks we experience along the way—if only *that person* would've done this, I would be manager by now! If we idolize image, we hate people who critique us and people who look better than we do.

Hatred marks the life of those who don't know Christ—they're hateful and hating each other. Relationships are marred by vendettas and agendas as people use one another to achieve whatever goal they think will fulfill the longing deep within their souls.

Apart from Christ is a desolate place to be. We were **foolish**, completely ignorant of God and truth. We were **disobedient**, with even our best deeds marred by sin and selfish motivations. We were **deceived** by Satan himself, thinking we're not that bad, or that our get-out-of-hell-free card ensures that we're fine, even if we do nothing else of eternal significance here on earth. We're **enslaved to various lusts and pleasures** we once enjoyed, before they gripped us in the unrelenting claws of death that stole our hope of freedom. We spent our lives in **malice and envy**, internal and horrendous sins that aggravated our souls and disrupted our relationships. And finally, we were **hateful and hating one another** when they couldn't fulfill us as we thought they should. We were destitute, hopeless, and far worse off than even our depraved minds could comprehend.

BUT WHEN THE KINDNESS OF GOD OUR SAVIOR AND HIS LOVE FOR MANKIND APPEARED ...

One of my favorite words in the entire Bible is "but." My pastor in college preached an entire sermon series on that single word, and it was so profound I'll never forget it. Why is it so awe-inspiring? Because it represents God's divine intervention in our lives. Paul has just finished writing how miserable we are in sin—hopelessly lost, utterly alone. And we would've stayed that way forever, **but** God decided to intervene. In the midst of utter despair, God stepped in and thwarted Satan's plan. Sin doesn't have the last word; God does. And He speaks it often in His Word with the simple conjunction, **but.**

The intense downward spiral of evil in our lives was interrupted **when the kindness of God our Savior and His love for mankind appeared.** Paul has already written that **the grace of God has appeared.** Now he emphasizes two other aspects of God's motivation to save us: His **kindness** and **love for us.** We don't often discuss God's **kindness**, to our loss. It means God's "generosity and goodness, especially toward humanity and for humanity's benefit."[268] Interestingly, it's also an exclusively Pauline term in the New Testament, some examples including:[269]

> Or do you think lightly of the riches of His kindness and tolerance and patience, not knowing that the **kindness** of God leads you to repentance?[270]

> So that in the ages to come He might show the surpassing riches of His grace in **kindness** toward us in Christ Jesus.[271]

> So, as those who have been chosen of God, holy and beloved, put on a heart of compassion, **kindness**, humility, gentleness and patience.[272]

God's **kindness** motivated Him to save just as it motivates us to receive it. It appeared with Christ and continues to appear as a fruit of the Spirit in the lives of those who believe.

A far more popular aspect of God is **His love.** But this is a unique reference to it. The exact rendition of this Greek word for love is seen only twice in the New Testament, and "only here in reference to God's character."[273] Paul is implementing a double meaning here with the terms **kindness** and **love,** for "both terms describe virtues that ought to characterize rulers as they relate to their subjects, and belonged to the vocabulary current in the Imperial cult and its worship."[274] Paul used a wide spectrum of apologetics in his evangelization. He often used pagan traditions, philosophies, and archetypes to introduce a truth about God, then he explained how God is the ultimate fulfillment of truth and all its manifestations. He did whatever he could to find a connection with unbelievers so that he could share the gospel with them:

> For though I am free from all men, I have made myself a slave to all, so that I may win more. To the Jews I became as a Jew, so that I might win Jews; to those who are under the Law, as under the Law though not being myself under the Law, so that I might win those who are under the Law; to those who are without law, as without law, though not being without the law of God but under the law of Christ, so that I might win those who are without law. To the weak I became weak, that I might win the weak; I have become all things to all men, so that I may by all means save some. I do all things for the sake of the gospel.[275]

While Titus (a strong believer) is the recipient of the letter, Paul knows Titus will share the truths written. He might additionally be imparting evangelistic ideas to Titus in the way he communicates these truths about God. Regardless, he wants us to know that God deals with our sin through His **kindness** and **love.**

HE SAVED US, NOT ON THE BASIS OF DEEDS WHICH WE HAVE DONE IN RIGHTEOUSNESS,

God broke into the sin-infested world that abhorred Him and **saved us.** This action is the climax of this passage (as well as our lives), for everything prior points to our dire need of it, and everything following provides a greater explanation of it. It's the gospel—the crux of eternal life, the most glorious and powerful "**but**" the world could ever hope to know.

Paul reminds us that our salvation is **not on the basis of deeds which we have done in righteousness,** because as he's already said, we are incapable of doing any good deeds in our previous **foolish, disobedient, deceived, enslaved,** and **hateful** condition. Prior to Christ, righteousness eludes us completely; all our works are stained by the sin that keeps us from God:

> For all of us have become like one who is unclean, and all our righteous deeds are like a filthy garment; and all of us wither like a leaf, and our iniquities, like the wind, take us away.[276]

This can be difficult to comprehend, for surely we're capable of doing *some* good apart from Christ. Consider nonprofits who perhaps aren't Christian organizations, yet are doing a lot of good for the world—defending domestic violence victims, sheltering the homeless, feeding the hungry, or distributing desperately needed vaccines free of charge to those who can't afford them. While these are technically good, they hold no eternal value; any reward received for performing the action is received in this world, not the next. Why? Because their motives are impure.

> Beware of practicing your righteousness before men to be noticed by them; otherwise you have no reward with your Father who is in heaven. So when you give to the poor, do not sound a trumpet before you, as the hypocrites do in the synagogues and in the streets, so that they may be honored by men. Truly I say to you, they have their reward in full. But when you give to the poor, do not let your left hand know what your right hand is doing, so

that your giving will be in secret; and your Father who sees what
is done in secret will reward you.[277]

If the motivation is wrong, any reward for good works is received in full on earth. But we shouldn't let the location of the reward distract us from even more dangerous ramifications. If good works are not done from a gospel perspective and motivation, they aren't merely hollow. They may actually keep the individual from God. Yes, good deeds can keep people from God when they think they're drawing closer to Him. Yet another one of Satan's great deceptions.

The best example of this is the story of the Prodigal Sons in the gospel of Luke.[278] In it, a man had two sons, neither of whom loved him. The younger son demanded his inheritance before his father died (a major offense in ancient cultures, since it meant he wished his father dead) to go and live as he wanted, outside his father's control. He lived it up and had a blast until he ended up broke, hungry, and a companion of swine. He realized his mistake, humbled himself, and returned home, hoping to become his father's slave, since even the household servants lived better than he did. Unbeknownst to him, the father had been watching and waiting for him daily, despite having zero evidence he would ever return. Upon seeing him, the father ran to greet him (also unheard of, for grown, esteemed men did not run). The father embraced his son and restored him fully to the family, celebrating by throwing a huge feast.

The other son did everything by the book, contrary to his younger brother. He kept all the rules, obeyed all the laws, and made sure his good deeds outweighed his bad. When his younger brother returned home, the older was livid and refused to attend the party, despite his father's pleas. He didn't want to forgive his brother, didn't understand why his father forgave his brother, and certainly didn't understand why his return was being celebrated. Instead of rejoicing with the rest of the household, he sulked. Badly. He had done everything right, but the younger, erroneous, wayward brother was being celebrated.

Not only that, but now his inheritance would be cut. The assets that remained, after the younger brother squandered his inheritance, would inevitably belong to the elder brother, to be fully collected when their father died. By being restored to the family, the younger brother would once again receive an inheritance, which would be taken from the elder brother's portion.

Both sons were wrong, both sons were lost, and both sons were seeking salvation from their own vantage points. The younger son went to the world to try to find himself. He was rebellious and exactly what most of us would think of when we think of someone being spiritually lost. The elder brother, who was just as lost, looks a whole lot like the majority of church congregations on Sunday mornings—doing everything "right," volunteering and participating in all kinds of wonderful deeds that earn them gold stars in the church world. These good deeds, however, were rubbish. His "righteousness" was nothing but a cleverly designed façade to pride. The elder brother was angry when his father restored his younger brother, and here's why:

> He feels he has the right to tell the father how the robes, rings, and livestock of the family should be deployed. In the same way, religious people commonly live very moral lives, but their goal is to get leverage over God, to control him, to put him in a position where they think he owes them. Therefore, despite all their ethical fastidiousness and piety, they are actually rebelling against his authority … If, like the elder brother, you seek to control God through your obedience, then all your morality is just a way to use God to make him give you the things in life you really want.[279]

The older brother was just as far from God as his wayward younger brother, even though his life looked the picture of religious piety. His good deeds acted as a buffer, keeping him further from God, because he was using them for ulterior motives. Neither son loved the father. They merely used him as a means to an end. The same can be said for anyone filling their lives with good **deeds**, hoping they'll lead to salvation. Works are never a way to attain a right standing with God, and Paul reminds Titus (and thereby, the Cretan Christians) of this. Rather, good works are the byproduct of a life gripped to the core with the gospel of Jesus Christ.

BUT ACCORDING TO HIS MERCY

God accomplished salvation **not on the basis of deeds which we have done in righteousness, but according to His mercy.** Another brilliant **but** for us. While we were utterly lost, trusting in a broken compass of self-serving morals, God intervened. He knew our location the entire time and decided to have **mercy**, although we didn't deserve a second glance.

Mercy differs from the grace Paul mentioned before. While grace is unmerited favor, **mercy** is a pardon. Grace is getting something we don't deserve; mercy is not getting something we do deserve. We deserve hell. Our sins demand the payment of God's eternal judgment and righteous wrath. Because of our **foolish, disobedient, deceived, enslaved, malice- and envy-**filled, **hateful** selves, we deserve nothing but to rot in abysmal, unrelenting torment for all eternity. We stand guilty before the Judge, knowing what we deserve and where our souls are headed. **But** Jesus. Jesus enters the courtroom, tells the Judge He will pay our debt by suffering God's excruciating and just wrath on our behalf. He extends **mercy** to us by enduring what we deserve.

Salvation is just as much an act of **mercy** as it is grace. And oh, how our hearts rejoice (and bow in overwhelmed gratitude) just thinking about it.

BY THE WASHING OF REGENERATION AND RENEWING BY THE HOLY SPIRIT, WHOM HE POURED OUT UPON US RICHLY THROUGH JESUS CHRIST OUR SAVIOR

If salvation is the *what* of this passage, Paul now gives us the *how*. As an act of His **mercy,** we are washed with regeneration and renewed by the Holy Spirit. Interpreting the structure of this phrase is not easy, because we're not sure where grammatical breaks are made in the original Greek. Is it two separate actions—**the washing of regeneration** standing on its own apart from the **renewing by the Holy Spirit**? Or does the **Holy Spirit** wash believers with both **regeneration and renewing**? Not an easy one to determine, but the more probable translation is that the agent of the washing is the Holy Spirit, and the washing produces both regeneration and renewal. Or in a crude analogy, the Holy Spirit is the employee working the car wash, the process of the car getting clean is the washing, and the result of the car getting clean is the regeneration and renewal. One agent/employee, one wash, two results.

The term **washing** is far less mysterious. It means to cleanse or make clean, and is found all over both Old and New Testaments. **Washing** in the Old Testament was a ritual required to be considered "clean" before God. People couldn't approach God or offer sacrifices to temporarily atone for their sins if they weren't first clean.[280] It was symbolic, of course, because external cleanliness doesn't make a soul clean. But it was necessary, and a good reminder of one's status before God.

In the New Testament, **washing** took on a whole new meaning with baptism. Baptism (*baptizma,* full immersion into water) is symbolic of salvation—dying, being buried, and rising again with Christ:

> Or do you not know that all of us who have been baptized into Christ Jesus have been baptized into His death? Therefore we have been buried with Him through baptism into death, so that as Christ was raised from the dead through the glory of the Father, so we too might walk in newness of life. For if we have become united with Him in the likeness of His death, certainly we shall also be in the likeness of His resurrection, knowing this,

that our old self was crucified with Him, in order that our body of sin might be done away with, so that we would no longer be slaves to sin; for he who has died is freed from sin. Now if we have died with Christ, we believe that we shall also live with Him, knowing that Christ, having been raised from the dead, is never to die again; death no longer is master over Him. For the death that He died, He died to sin once and for all; but the life that He lives, He lives to God. Even so consider yourselves to be dead to sin, but alive to God in Christ Jesus.[281]

Just as baptism signifies the cleansing we receive with salvation, **washing … by the Holy Spirit** is also symbolic of the cleansing that saves us. This is most likely not a direct reference to baptism, but rather, *like* baptism, stands symbolic of a greater theological truth.[282]

Regeneration is also translated rebirth and means "a radical new beginning, since 'God has not repaired us, but has made us all new.'"[283] The idea of being born again or made new in salvation is familiar and originated with Jesus:

Jesus answered and said to him, "Truly, truly, I say to you, unless one is born again he cannot see the kingdom of God." Nicodemus said to Him, "How can a man be born when he is old? He cannot enter a second time into his mother's womb and be born, can he?" Jesus answered, "Truly, truly, I say to you, unless one is born of water and the Spirit he cannot enter into the kingdom of God. That which is born of the flesh is flesh, and that which is born of the Spirit is spirit. Do not be amazed that I said to you, 'You must be born again.'"[284]

When we are born of God, we are regenerated—experiencing a new birth into the family of God. No longer bound to our lives of sin, we start fresh and embrace life in our new identities in Christ. This is one of the Holy

Spirit's many contributions to the enactment of salvation in our lives, as is **renewing.**

Renewing refers "to an internal change, which in this context may suggest a process begun within the believer from the moment of conversion." The only other time this exact Greek word (*anakainosis*), is used is in Paul's letter to the Romans:

> And do not be conformed to this world, but be transformed by the **renewing** of your mind, so that you may prove what the will of God is, that which is good and acceptable and perfect.[285]

When we accept Christ, we are made new from the inside out and are changed. This change begins immediately, but is continually worked out by the Holy Spirit and our participation with Him via spiritual disciplines and wise choices. The Holy Spirit carries out the process, but our willing and diligent cooperation serves as added fuel as He renews and transforms us into the image of our Savior.

The agent of these aspects of salvation is, as we've mentioned, **the Holy Spirit, whom He poured out upon us richly through Jesus Christ our Savior.** The Holy Spirit is the least-known and least-understood member of the Trinity, but is just as important, worthy, and vital to the Godhead as the Father and Jesus Christ. For the sake of being thorough, let's do a brief walkthrough of pneumatology, the study of the Holy Spirit.

The Holy Spirit is a person, like God the Father and Jesus Christ. He is not some ethereal blob that moves around wherever the wind blows Him. When described in Scripture, the male pronoun is always used rather than the gender-neutral one, confirming His individuality. He also is deity (fully God) as an equal member of the Godhead Trinity. He executes ministry alongside the Father and Christ, though with His own unique role. Before Christ, He was involved in creating the world and empowered and enabled specific individuals for certain roles as they carried out God's will. His presence was temporary in their lives, but just as potent as it is for believers today. He also played a vital role in keeping sin restrained in the world, and aided in the process of revealing prophecies to individuals and then within the pages of Scripture.

During Christ's ministry, we see much evidence of the Holy Spirit's ministry. The incarnation of Christ was His doing, and we see His presence at Christ's birth, baptism, temptations, ministry, miracles, and empowerment in general. He brought Christ glory and worked to confirm Jesus as having come from God.

His ministry today is most elaborately known; this is, after all, the age of the Holy Spirit. Upon accepting Christ as our Savior, God pours out the Holy Spirit **upon us richly through Jesus Christ our Savior.** All three members of the Godhead are mentioned in this brief phrase, making it a powerful declaration of this component of salvation. When we are saved, we receive the Holy Spirit as a permanent companion to our souls. He indwells us, first by sealing us into God's family and serving as a pledge for us as security in Christ:

> In Him, you also, after listening to the message of truth, the
> gospel of your salvation—having also believed, you were sealed
> in Him with the Holy Spirit of promise, who is given as a pledge
> of our inheritance, with a view to the redemption of God's own
> possession, to the praise of His glory.[286]

God doesn't hold back in this gift of the Spirit; neither does the Spirit in His ministry to us. He actively illuminates Scripture in our minds, aids in our prayers, and transforms us into Christ's image as He endows us with spiritual gifts. God the Father, Christ the Son, and the Holy Spirit are equal members of the Godhead Trinity, all serving unique roles to enact the gospel in the world and in our individual lives.

SO THAT BEING JUSTIFIED BY HIS GRACE WE WOULD BE MADE HEIRS ACCORDING TO THE HOPE OF ETERNAL LIFE.

Salvation is the *what*, regeneration and renewing by the Holy Spirit is the *how*, and now Paul tells us the *why*—**so that being justified by His grace we would be made heirs according to the hope of eternal life.** God makes us a literal and permanent part of His family, destined to experience eternal life with Him and all His revealing glory. Our status as His begins now, and while it's not perfect, we do receive glimpses of glory in our individual faith experiences as well as when we are together with other family members (i.e., the church).

This inclusion into His family begins by **being justified by His grace.** Justification is a major tenant of faith, and it means to be placed in a right standing with God, just as if we'd never sinned.

Justification before God is two-fold. On the one hand, it means we are declared, accepted, and treated as not guilty; on the other hand, we are "entitled to all the privileges due to those who have kept the law."[287] Back to the courtroom analogy. Our sins made us unquestionably guilty and deserving of full punishment. But when Christ substituted Himself for us, God, the Judge, made a pronouncement of our new position: not guilty. He reinstated us to life and society, as if we'd kept the law the whole time. This is justification. It's the pronouncement of our new, not-guilty-and-receipient-of-every-blessing-fathomable-including-eternal-life-in-everlasting-glory position declared by God Himself. And, as Paul reminded us earlier, He cannot lie.

The God of the universe announced and confirmed our justified status. We can't change it or mess it up, because we didn't attain it or earn it. Nor do we sustain our justification by our actions. It originates and is preserved entirely by God. We can embrace it and live it out (which the letter to Titus is all about), or we can let it collect dust on our souls as we waste our time on earth until we meet Jesus.

We are **justified by His grace,** meaning once again, that we received justification, having done nothing to deserve it.

> For of His fullness, we have all received, and grace upon grace.[288]

That sums it up. Our entire lives in Christ can be defined as receiving grace upon grace. Just when we think there couldn't possibly be more to discover, He proves us wrong by revealing yet another astounding aspect of His grace in our lives. The gospel is endless in its truth. We could dedicate our entire lives to its study, only to scratch the surface. Good thing our journey only begins on earth as we are **made heirs according to the hope of eternal life.**

Being **made heirs** is a pretty big deal, because it means we stand with Christ as God's children. Christ becomes our elder brother, but unlike the elder brother prodigal son, Christ is our true elder brother who loves us and willingly gave all He had to bring the wayward younger brother (us) back home.

> The younger son gets a Pharisee for a brother … we do not. By putting a flawed elder brother in the story, Jesus is inviting us to imagine and yearn for a true one. And we have Him. Think of the kind of brother we need. We need one who does not just go to the next country to find us but who will come all the way from heaven to earth. We need one who is willing to pay not just a finite amount of money, but, at the infinite cost of his own life to bring us into God's family, for our debt is so much greater.[289]

> The Spirit Himself testifies with our spirit that we are children of God, and if children, heirs also, heirs of God and fellow heirs with Christ …[290]

Jesus is our true elder brother, and we stand with Him as **heirs according to the hope of eternal life.** Paul has already written about the blessed hope we are looking for when Jesus comes again. Hope is sure, steadfast, and God's promise, which cannot be broken. We also experience **hope of eternal life.**

We have received eternal life now in Christ by faith, but we won't realize it fully until we are released from this life and ushered into heaven with Him. By "becoming 'heirs' (through salvation), Christians become possessors of a guaranteed future referred to as 'the hope of eternal life.'"[291] Eternal life is experienced in part now, and the glimpses are enough to satisfy us for a thousand lifetimes. But **the hope of eternal life** that is to come will make even the most weighty glimpses here seem puny.

One of my prayers is for God to reveal Himself so profoundly to me here that, when I see Him face to face for the first time (after peeling myself off the ground in worship), I will say, "I *knew* it. I *knew* You—the nuances of Your beauty, the details of Your character, the gleam in Your eye when You look at me ..." While I'll be floored, I yearn for at least a part of me not to be surprised. That's how deeply I long to know Him, and just a fraction of how much He desires to be known.

THIS IS A TRUSTWORTHY STATEMENT; AND CONCERNING THESE THINGS I WANT YOU TO SPEAK CONFIDENTLY, SO THAT THOSE WHO HAVE BELIEVED GOD WILL BE CAREFUL TO ENGAGE IN GOOD DEEDS. THESE THINGS ARE GOOD AND PROFITABLE FOR MEN.

The **trustworthy statement** Paul refers to here includes all the material discussed in this section thus far, verses 1-7 of chapter 3. Paul knows his theology and knows it's trustworthy, because God revealed it to him. God confirmed its truth by incorporating it into the canon of Scripture, for "all Scripture is inspired by God and profitable for teaching, for reproof, for correction, for training in righteousness."[292]

Paul once again expresses his desire for Titus **to speak** in accordance with truth, this time adding the adverb **confidently**, just in case Titus has any reservations. We trust our eternal destinies to God's truth. We can speak confidently of it, as Titus did to the Cretan believers.

The reason Paul wants Titus to remind believers of these truths is so they **will be careful to engage in good deeds.** Again, truth by itself isn't enough for life transformation. We must practice and exercise truth before it will be realized in our lives. The purpose of knowing truth isn't to increase our intellectual prowess, but to give us ammunition against the enemy and the fleshly desires we were once enslaved to. Paul's letter has been drenched in this fact. Elders were men who lived above reproach. Older and younger men, older and young women, and bondslaves were to live out their faith, each in their respective ways. Titus was to lead by example, allowing his faith to come alive so others would do likewise. All good works, of course, were to be motivated by the gospel, performed in response to all Christ has done for us, not in an attempt to attain good standing with God. Such motivational truth inspires behavior that reflects it—submission and obedience to authorities, wishing no one harm, and treating others well. Paul knew Titus and the Cretan Christians (like any and every other Christian) needed to be reminded of the truth over and over again, so their motivation would be renewed and they would thrive in lives characterized by good works.

All **these things are good and profitable for men.** Our spiritual health and well-being depend on not only knowing truth, but living it out. For our **good,** God reveals His gospel, saves us, then teaches us how to unleash its power in our lives. It is also **profitable** for everyone; "**men**" refers to mankind in general, not just the male population. **Profitable**, in a spiritual sense, doesn't necessarily mean profitable in a worldly sense (we probably won't accumulate physical wealth by knowing and living out truth), but we will accrue immeasurable riches where the world can't touch it—in our status, relationship, and future with God in Christ.

The only way to fully embrace and experience life on earth in a manner worthy of our future lives in heaven is to be reminded of the gospel—

God's plan to rescue a spiritually dead, broken, condemned, and sin-enslaved world, giving eternal life and restoring it to peace with Him through the comprehensive and final sacrifice of Jesus Christ—who was born of a virgin, lived a sinless life, died on the cross, was buried, and rose again—bringing us to life in Him, adopting us into His family, and securing us in His glorious future.

We need to remember who we were prior to Christ, what Christ has accomplished on our behalf, what our future looks like in Him, and how we're supposed to engage in good works in the meantime. By constantly remembering, we'll become so absorbed in the gospel that we will hardly remember life before it. We are His, and our lives are to reflect that fact in knowledge, word, and deed.

GROUP STUDY

INTRODUCTION

Memory is a powerful tool wielded by wise men and fools alike.

To remember is to pause and reflect, if only for a moment, to evaluate a past situation and glean lessons from it. Wisdom calls us to be intentional with memory—remembering in order to accomplish something (avoiding similar mistakes, learning from previous choices, etc.) But we can also be foolish with our memories, coloring them to reflect imagination more than fact, or even becoming so obsessed with them that we refuse to leave.

- How have you "colored" a past memory to make it better or worse than it actually was?

- Share a memory you've learned a lot from, either yours or someone else's.

THE WORD

Paul realized that believers needed to remember truth if they had any hope of living it out. Thus, he instructs Titus to "remind them" of it, purposefully and consistently. Truth didn't stop with showing them how they should act. It also showed them where they came from and how Christ stepped in to give them life so they could exercise wisdom in their behavior.

> Remind them to be subject to rulers, to authorities, to be obedient, to be ready for every good deed, to malign no one, to be peaceable, gentle, showing every consideration for all men. (Titus 3:1-2)

For we also once were foolish ourselves, disobedient, deceived, enslaved to various lusts and pleasures, spending our life in malice and envy, hateful, hating one another. (Titus 3:3)

But when the kindness of God our Savior and His love for mankind appeared, He saved us, not on the basis of deeds which we have done in righteousness, but according to His mercy, by the washing of regeneration and renewing by the Holy Spirit, whom He poured out upon us richly through Jesus Christ our Savior, so that being justified by His grace we would be made heirs according to the hope of eternal life. (Titus 3:4-7)

This is a trustworthy statement; and concerning these things I want you to speak confidently, so that those who have believed God will be careful to engage in good deeds. These things are good and profitable for men. (Titus 3:8)

- Who were Cretan Christians supposed to be subject to (3:1)?

  - Why can that be difficult for people, especially the church?

- How does the Bible describe us, prior to our salvation (3:3)?

  - _____

  - _____

  - _____

  - _____

  - _____

  - _____

  - _____

- Are any of these surprising to you? How so?

- What is salvation *not* based on (3:4-7)?

  - Why is that important?

- Name two aspects of the Holy Spirit's role in salvation (3:4-7).

  Washing of _____ and _____

  - What do those mean?

- What are we made after being justified in His grace (3:4-7)?

  - Why is that a big deal?

APPLY

As justified people still living in a broken world, we will always wrestle with past desires and tendencies. But we have more than we need to overcome them, beginning with the simple practice of remembering who we are and what God has done for us.

"These things I have spoken to you, so that in Me you may have peace. In the world you have tribulation, but take courage; I have overcome the world."
Jesus, John 16:33

"But the Helper, the Holy Spirit, whom the Father will send in My name, He will teach you all things, and bring to your remembrance all that I said to you."
Jesus, John 14:26

A unique aspect of remembrance in the Christian realm is the fact that we remember not just the past (ours and what God has done), but also the truths that impact our present and future lives.

- Does any aspect of your past hold you in bondage (or negatively influence you) right now?

  - What truth(s) do you need to remember in order to combat and overcome it?

- In what ways do you tend to forget that God is active and present (or wants to be) in your life right now?

- How much influence does your future (in heaven as God's heir) have on your daily life?

  - In what ways do you think it should serve as greater motivation for how you live now?

WEEK SIX
TITUS 3:9-15

PERSONAL BIBLE STUDY QUESTIONS

1. What was Titus (and Cretan Christians by extension) supposed to avoid? (3:9)

    a)

    b)

    c)

    d)

2. Why were they supposed to avoid them? (3:9)

3. How many warnings was a factious man to receive? (3:10)

4. Why was he to be rejected after those warnings? (3:11)

5. Who was Paul sending to Titus? (3:12)

6. What did Paul want Titus to do when they arrived? (3:12)

7. What must "our people" also learn to do? (3:14)

8. Why was it important? (3:14)

9. Why do you think being greeted by "all who are with" Paul would've been important to Titus? (3:15)

COMMENTARY

But avoid foolish controversies and genealogies and strife and disputes about the Law, for they are unprofitable and worthless. Reject a factious man after a first and second warning, knowing that such a man is perverted and is sinning, being self-condemned. When I send Artemas or Tychicus to you, make every effort to come to me at Nicopolis, for I have decided to spend the winter there. Diligently help Zenas the lawyer and Apollos on their way so that nothing is lacking for them. Our people must also learn to engage in good deeds to meet pressing needs, so that they will not be unfruitful. All who are with me greet you. Greet those who love us in the faith.

Titus 3:9-15

Community detonates explosive growth in our lives. God designed us to live in close fellowship with one another, which enables us to thrive in our faith in ways we never could've achieved on our own. Healthy faith requires constant learning and striving for more of God. This is best done in the context of relationships—both with God and with one another.

Paul understood the importance of deep fellowship among ministry workers. Titus was, in a sense, stranded and theologically isolated on an island. This knowledge pushed Paul to send reminders of the importance of his task, along with reminders that Titus wasn't alone. His letter to Titus is an extension of such concern, and Paul also sent other ministry help to boost Titus' morale and to aid in the extensive gospel work he was accomplishing in Crete. Paul's final words to Titus in this letter reflect his zeal for community, wanting Titus to receive last morsels of instruction along with the rejuvenation of spirit that comes with genuine and thriving fellowship.

BUT AVOID FOOLISH CONTROVERSIES AND GENEALOGIES AND STRIFE
AND DISPUTES ABOUT THE LAW, FOR THEY ARE UNPROFITABLE AND
WORTHLESS.

Lots of things threaten the rooting of solid doctrine in our lives. Irrelevant theological pursuits choke any beneficial roots right out. Yes, some theological (the study of God) pursuits hinder or even stop personal growth. While interesting to ponder, certain aspects of religious studies serve only to distract people from focusing on explicit doctrine that brings life.

Some topics fitting this category today are biblical numerology (assigning numerical values to the ancient texts of Scripture for "deeper" interpretation), obsessing over the end times, a preoccupation with the spiritual world of angels and demons, etc. While every truth presented in Scripture is important, we sometimes get so caught up in details (and arguments) about them that we miss their point and what they're there to show us: Christ and the gospel. Not only can such pursuits become giant wastes of time, but they also interrupt fellowship and can cause major schisms in the church.

Cretan believers had succumbed to the same temptation. Paul has already mentioned this earlier in the letter, when describing the rebellious men who were "empty talkers and deceivers," men far more interested in "Jewish myths and commandments" than they were in Christology, which resulted in turning "people away from the truth" and causing disruption of fellowship in the church. Knowing the seriousness of the threat, Paul reminds Titus once again to **avoid foolish controversies and genealogies and strife and disputes about the law.**

At the time, "apparently some Hellenistic Jews on Crete, who had 'accepted Christ,' were also promoting continuing connections with Judaism, especially in the form of speculative teaching and rigorous devotion to rules and regulations."[293] In essence, they had added Christ to their pre-established understanding of theology, rather than replacing former doctrine with Christ and gospel alone.

This was not new, nor was it limited to Crete. Timothy, another mentee of Paul who served at Ephesus, dealt with the same threats to doctrine and fellowship:

> But refuse foolish and ignorant speculations, knowing that they produce quarrels.[294]

> If anyone advocates a different doctrine and does not agree with sound words, those of our Lord Jesus Christ, and with the doctrine conforming to godliness, he is conceited and understands nothing; but he has a morbid interest in controversial questions and disputes about words, out of which arise envy, strife, abusive language, evil suspicions, and constant friction between men of depraved mind and deprived of the truth, who suppose that godliness is a means of gain.[295]

> You may instruct certain men not to teach strange doctrines, nor to pay attention to myths and endless genealogies, which give rise to mere speculation rather than furthering the administration of God which is by faith.[296]

> But avoid worldly and empty chatter, for it will lead to further ungodliness.[297]

> Remind them of these things, and solemnly charge them in the presence of God not to wrangle about words, which is useless and leads to the ruin of the hearers.[298]

The church was new, impressionable, and easily led astray. Empty speculations would've been difficult for new believers to decipher as they learned correct doctrine, which made the threat that much more real.

Foolish controversies can encompass a broad spectrum of pointless banter, but this particular reference describes how things were discussed, but not necessarily the quality of the content.[299] The "adjective 'foolish' labels the theological inquiries as frivolous and incompetent, apparently because they produced no worthwhile results."[300] This would be similar to modern-day endless debates on the end times. Revelation is no less a part of the canon than any other, but the church is guilty of arguing about different translations of minute points about how the end times will unfold. This is utterly **foolish** because we simply aren't at liberty to know all the details with confidence. If God wanted us to know everything about the unfolding of the end times, He would've told us in a way that left no uncertainty. But He didn't. This should cause us to pause and consider the theological truths He does present clearly in the book.[301] Exploring it out of curiosity poses no issue; obsessing over it to the point of arguing with others and igniting friction in the church absolutely does.

Genealogies are as **foolish** to pursue as irrelevant controversies. Family lines were a much bigger part of society then than they are now (though they seem to be making a comeback with our culture wanting to know their ancestries). Consider Matthew, who begins his gospel with Jesus' genealogy, tracing His line all the way back to Abraham.[302] The Jewish religion prioritized bloodline, which made genealogies very important, especially for Jesus, who was fulfilling prophecies through His. Being a literal descendant of Abraham was paramount in their minds; whereas Christ said that His blood was the sacrifice that made physical bloodlines irrelevant in the kingdom of God.

The problem with **genealogies** arose when the Jewish Christians began making doctrinal interpretations in light of extraneous genealogical factors.

Thus, Paul's specific reference here is likely "a Jewish type of interpretation based on Old Testament and extra-canonical stories of the biblical heroes and speculation based on family trees."[303] The Jews held national historical conjecture on the same plane as Scripture by using genealogies found within them to interpret Scripture. Scripture stands alone. We're to uphold it, add nothing to it, and subject ourselves fully to its authority.

Foolish controversies and genealogies are not only fruitless, but they also produce ominous consequences, especially within church communities. The first consequence Paul notes is **strife**—quarreling and even all-out fighting in the church.[304] Since the mark of Christianity is one of love, **strife** has absolutely no part in the church. Christ was clear:

> A new commandment I give to you, that you love one another, even as I have loved you, that you also love one another. By this all men will know that you are My disciples, if you have love for one another.[305]

> This is My commandment, that you love one another, just as I have loved you.[306]

It's difficult to love each other when we're fighting, bickering, and disagreeing with one another, especially over utterly ridiculous and superficial issues. If ever our discussion turns hostile, we must stop. Take a breath, step away, reevaluate, refocus perspective. While we may have to reassess a relationship with someone who doesn't hold to sound doctrine, no relationship is worth sacrificing over **foolish** religious pursuits.

Lastly, Paul teaches us to evade **disputes about the Law**. This instruction "alludes to heated arguments about [the] Torah," which is the first five books of the Old Testament.[307] We're not sure what specific disputes entailed, but because of the deep-seeded nature of Judaism, we can imagine that their tangents and disputes were endless.

All these disrupting behaviors—**foolish controversies and genealogies and strife and disputes about the Law**—were dangerous because of their **unprofitable and worthless** nature. These false teachings were "utterly wanting in the practical element which so remarkably characterizes the true doctrine of the gospel."[308] By striving for control, these Hellenistic Jews implemented impractical rules and proposed theories of behavior and doctrine, not realizing the gospel was all they needed. Such speculations were **unprofitable and worthless. Unprofitable** because absolutely nothing good benefited from their exploration; **worthless** because they distracted people from the gospel.

It must have been tempting, at least in part, for Titus to partake in such conversations, if only to prove them wrong. Debates can be quite entertaining, and in a highly oral culture, such activities could draw attention. Titus was armed with the truth of God's Word, able to squelch even the most potent lies, but Paul knew that such attempts, especially in regard to these particular controversies, would be futile. Some people, after all, are interested only in arguing and creating drama, since they have no interest in changing their minds. Titus was to speak the truth and reprove those who directly argued against it, but avoid topics and situations that were **unprofitable and worthless,** especially because of their penchant to disrupt unity in the church.

REJECT A FACTIOUS MAN AFTER A FIRST AND SECOND WARNING, KNOWING THAT SUCH A MAN IS PERVERTED AND IS SINNING, BEING SELF-CONDEMNED.

Along with avoiding insoluble intellectual controversies, Titus was to **reject a factious man after a first and second warning, knowing that such a man is perverted and is sinning, being self-condemned.** A **factious** (*hairetikos*) man is contentious or divisive.[309] Some have translated this word as "heretic," "but that is to read later ideas back into the text."[310] While this term did come to mean heretic as years progressed, it hadn't yet made that transformation when this text was written; thus, sticking with the original meaning of contentious or divisive is best.

This kind of individual was a serious threat to the church, which was already under attack by false teachers and doctrine. Satan loves to cause friction and create schisms within the church, because he knows how powerful unity is among believers. God is the complete and perfect example of unity, and He yearns for us to be incorporated into His fellowship:

> For their sakes I sanctify Myself, that they themselves also may be sanctified in truth. I do not ask on behalf of these alone, but for those also who believe in Me through their word; that they may all be one; even as You, Father, are in Me and I in You, that they also may be in Us, so that the world may believe that You sent Me. The glory which You have given Me I have given to them, that they may be one, just as We are one; I in them and You in Me, that they may be perfected in unity, so that the world may know that You sent Me, and loved them, even as You have loved Me.[311]

When that unity is broken, it creates catastrophic effects in the kingdom of God and keeps others from drawing near to Christ. As a major theme in this book (adorning the Word of God with our lives), Paul communicates once again how unacceptable such behavior is.

Even more horrendous are the things that tear us apart. We're not told exactly how these men were being **factious,** though it wouldn't at all be surprising if they were participating in the **foolish controversies and genealogies and strife and disputes about the Law** mentioned previously. Disagreements can begin over the simplest, stupidest things, like a misunderstanding, or something as frivolous as the color of the carpet in a church building today.

I served in a ministry for church health while working on my masters, and my immediate supervisor served as the director of the ministry. He worked with churches all over the nation as they struggled through splits and tensions, and he served as a mediator to get them back together and on the same ministry heartbeat once more. His stories are grotesquely depressing. Treating each other with contempt and hostility in the church is atrocious. But it happens every single day. And while churches are being planted daily, nearly as many are shutting their doors, mostly because of miniscule infractions that began over something completely irrelevant, weren't handled correctly, and then mushroomed into unresolvable catastrophes.

Any perpetrator of such friction was to be confronted and given **a first and second warning.** Paul wanted any and all disputes nipped in the bud so they wouldn't disrupt the unity of the church.

Warnings weren't simply verbal cautions or advice for a change in behavior. Rather, they "included instruction, correction, and warning with a view to regaining the offender … corrective teaching in the effort to convince the offender of the ethical or doctrinal error and win him/her back."[312] Just as Titus was to reprove false teachers severely "… so that they may be sound in the faith,"[313] he was also to distribute warnings to the same end.

However, if the divisive individual decided not to heed the warnings, Titus was to **reject** him. Any "further efforts would not be a good stewardship of his time and energies and would give the offender an underserved sense of importance."[314] To **reject** him meant "the severest sense of 'drive out, dismiss, discharge' … with excommunication from the church in view."[315] Such men wreaked havoc on churches, resulting "in believers who are confused, frustrated, angry, and hurt."[316] Such behavior was detrimental, and Paul wanted to empower Titus to take action against these people.

These people were **perverted, sinning,** and **self-condemned. Perverted** means corrupt or turned aside;[317] it's not a reference to a monster with gross sexual proclivities as it's typically used today. This individual is one who was perhaps walking on the right path of gospel-driven behavior, but somehow got turned aside and started heading in a direction contrary to it. In their corruptness they began leading others astray, which is one reason they must be rejected if they didn't repent.

Sinning is a straightforward reference meaning "that condition and activity of human beings that is offensive to God, their Creator."[318] We have all have "… sinned and fall short of the glory of God,"[319] but the individual Paul has in mind here is one who continues **sinning**, despite multiple warnings to stop.

Self-condemned is a literal translation of the Greek word *autokatakritos*, and this is the only time it is used in the New Testament. The idea behind its meaning is that "by his very persistence in his sinful behavior he has condemned himself, thus putting himself on the outside" of the church and what it stands for.[320] This person knows exactly what he is doing, and therefore, he condemns himself by his actions.

This process of confronting and rejecting an individual who sins directly mirrors Christ's instruction on the matter:

> If your brother sins, go and show him his fault in private; if he listens to you, you have won your brother. But if he does not listen to you, take one or two more with you, so that by the mouth of two or three witnesses every fact may be confirmed. If he refuses to listen to them, tell it to the church; and if he refuses to listen even to the church, let him be to you as a Gentile and a tax collector.[321]

The process is clearly defined. If someone notices sin within the church, he is to confront the guilty party in private first. This makes the situation far less volatile. Emotions are far easier to control, embarrassment is kept at a minimum, and the confronter can prayerfully consider words that can keep the guilty party from being threatened or intimidated. The guilty party is far less likely to feel attacked or defensive and is more likely to notice a genuine motivation behind the confronter's words.

If the erring individual reacts poorly to his brother's private reveal of sin, not listening to and then carrying on with his sin, the believer is to gather one or two witnesses and try again. The involvement of more people is, again, not to serve as an affront to the guilty person. They're not to attack or forcefully accuse out of spite or anger. Rather, they are to approach the person in love, confirming facts, walking the person through his sin. They should explain why it is wrong, how it harms the one sinning and others around him, and how to go about repentance and restoration.

If the guilty individual still refuses to listen, he is to be expelled from the body of believers. While excommunication is an intense punishment, it's not permanent. When Christ says to "let him be to you as a Gentile and a tax collector," He's not saying to ignore, hate, treat him poorly, and sever all ties with him and his family, in business and community alike. Quite the opposite. Christians are to love those outside the faith for the purpose of drawing them into the fold of faith. They were to love and show him God's kindness, praying that it would draw him to repentance. Full restoration with God and unity with the church body is the goal of any and every confrontation of sin.

WHEN I SEND ARTEMAS OR TYCHICUS TO YOU, MAKE EVERY EFFORT TO COME TO ME AT NICOPOLIS, FOR I HAVE DECIDED TO SPEND THE WINTER THERE.

After clarifying those points, Paul transitions to personal matters between himself and Titus. The first item on the agenda was a plea for Titus to come and visit him at the earliest practical opportunity. Since he knows the Cretan church isn't in a position to be left without theologically sound supervision, he planned to send either **Artemas** or **Tychicus** to provide relief for Titus.

Scripture mentions **Artemas** only here, meaning we don't know much about him at all. Non-Scriptural, historical tradition surmises that he was one of the seventy Jesus sent out to aid in His ministry, and that Artemas eventually became the first bishop of Lystra.[322] But that's not confirmed fact. We can, however, deduce from his name that he was Greek, which means he was grafted into the faith as a Gentile, not as a Jew (like Titus). We can also correctly estimate that he was a man of upstanding character, fully committed to the gospel work of which he was a minister. Paul wouldn't send someone questionable in morals or character to relieve Titus, particularly in a cultural environment saturated with horrendous morals. Whoever **Artemas** was, he was a good man and a solid candidate for providing Titus with ministerial relief so he could travel to Paul.

Tychicus is someone we know a little more about, for he's mentioned elsewhere in the New Testament:

> And he was accompanied by Sopater of Berea, the son of Pyrrhus, and by Aristarchus and Secundus of the Thessalonians, and Gaius of Derbe, and Timothy, and **Tychicus** and Trophimus of Asia.[323]

> But that you also may know about my circumstances, how I am doing, **Tychicus**, the beloved brother and faithful minister in the Lord, will make everything known to you.[324]

> As to all my affairs, **Tychicus**, our beloved brother and faithful servant and fellow bond-servant in the Lord, will bring you information.[325]

> But **Tychicus** I have sent to Ephesus.[326]

As with **Artemas, Tychicus'** name is Greek, meaning he came to faith as a Gentile, not a former Jew. Thus, he probably didn't need to be purged of the erroneous and intrinsically binding doctrines Jews had to shed in order to embrace Christ fully (though other pagan ideologies would've undoubtedly needed to be addressed). He also was a man of upstanding character, for he was a companion of Paul and was frequently trusted to carry out his ministry plans. He seems to have acted as Paul's emissary, traveling to different church bodies in order to update them on Paul's circumstances.[327] This infers that Paul trusted him as he did Titus, knowing he was a man of integrity and dependable to carry out any mission he received.

By calling him a "beloved brother," Paul reveals that he thought fondly of and loved **Tychicus**, viewing him as a brother in faith, as Titus was considered his "true child." Such references also suggest that Paul wanted the church to view and receive him that way as well. If Paul, a supreme authority figure in the early church, spoke highly of someone, that someone was to be received with utmost respect and admiration. Churches were probably eager to receive **Tychicus** as a direct representative of Paul.

Lastly, we can infer that **Tychicus,** like Titus and other ministry workers, put the advancement of the gospel over and above his personal comfort or pursuits. The gospel, in fact, was his ambition, and he yearned to carry it out in any way his spiritual elders (namely, Paul) saw fit. This reveals not only a humble spirit, but someone completely dedicated to the Lord.

Other New Testament letters don't tell us which disciple Paul ultimately chose to send, but we do know he sent someone, for he wanted Titus to come to him at **Nicopolis.**

Nicopolis, or "victory city," was Nicopolis of Epirus,[328] "a Roman colony on the western coast of Greece that served as provincial capital, having been founded by Augustus in 31-29 BC in order to celebrate his triumph over Mark Anthony at Actium."[329] It had existed well over fifty years by the time of Paul's writing to Titus and was a vital, well-known location for trade.[330] Paul desires to **winter there**, since it had a mild climate.[331] Travel from **Nicopolis** to Crete took five to ten days, since the distance between the two cities was more than three hundred miles.[332]

Paul had not yet arrived at **Nicopolis,** as we deduce from the verb tenses in the passage. He had **decided to spend the winter there** but hadn't yet arrived. Thus, Titus was to meet him there after having welcomed either **Artemas** or **Tychicus** to take over at Crete.

Paul's desire for Titus to come to him confirms Paul's affection and reveals another part of his ministry philosophy. He recognized the need for ministry leaders to get away from their current environment in order to rest and recharge. It's easy to get so immersed in a culture or project that we lose perspective or become so drained that we have nothing left to give. To prevent that, Paul wanted Titus to have time away so he could receive encouragement and ministry for a time.

This designated "away time" was purposeful and planned, not done on a whim. By writing this to Titus, Paul was beginning the plan and informing Titus so he could begin preparations on his end. While we're unsure of all it would require, it probably was quite an extensive endeavor for Titus, due to the size of his ministry on Crete. He'd need to prepare the already-instated elders in every city to gain confidence in their authority and ready themselves for his absence (though they would receive substitutional help from either Artemas or Tychicus). He'd need to gather information to give the substitute ministry worker, being ready to walk them through all the nuances of ministry on the island with individual house churches. Titus' ministry was intense (he was, after all, establishing the church there), so tidying everything up for a prolonged absence was probably complicated and in need of thorough planning.

Paul's wisdom extends from a deep understanding of the gospel and theology to ministry and how it's best carried out. He leads by example and refuses to use people for their skill sets, regardless of how impressive they are. Love and sincere dedication marked his relationships with other ministry workers, as he thought of them not as subordinates, but as family members to be respected and nurtured with utmost care.

DILIGENTLY HELP ZENAS THE LAWYER AND APOLLOS ON THEIR WAY SO THAT NOTHING IS LACKING FOR THEM. OUR PEOPLE MUST ALSO LEARN TO ENGAGE IN GOOD DEEDS TO MEET PRESSING NEEDS, SO THAT THEY WILL NOT BE UNFRUITFUL.

Paul's perspective no doubt filtered down to those who served with and under him. Just as he provides for them, he expects them to provide for one another with all eagerness and diligence. Two such people were **Zenas the lawyer and Apollos. Zenas the lawyer** isn't mentioned anywhere else in Scripture, but by his name and descriptive title, we can conclude that he was "either an expert in Jewish law or perhaps a Roman civil jurist."[333] Like **Artemas** and **Tychicus,** it's reasonable to assume he was in good standing with Paul, being a man of faith who exuded integrity and drive to see the gospel advanced in this world.

We know far more about **Apollos** than any of the other three ministry workers named in this passage. His first mention is in Acts:

> Now a Jew named **Apollos,** an Alexandrian by birth, an eloquent man, came to Ephesus; and he was mighty in the Scriptures. This man had been instructed in the way of the Lord; and being fervent in spirit, he was speaking and teaching accurately the things concerning Jesus, being acquainted only with the baptism of John; and he began to speak out boldly in the synagogue. But when Priscilla and Aquila heard him, they took him aside and explained to him the way of God more accurately. And when he

wanted to go across to Achaia, the brethren encouraged him and wrote to the disciples to welcome him; and when he had arrived, he greatly helped those who had believed through grace, for he powerfully refuted the Jews in public, demonstrating by the Scriptures that Jesus was the Christ.[334]

Apollos was quite the impressive man. He was Egyptian, and there's evidence that the Jewish community living on Crete at the time Titus was there was originally from Alexandria, Egypt. This gave Apollos a natural connection with the island.[335] Being bright and "instructed in the way of the Lord," he "boldly" shared the truth he knew. This says a lot about his character, for he was determined and committed to ministry, just as the other disciples.

Interestingly, this passage about **Apollos** gives us a beautiful example of confrontation. While he wasn't sinning, he was preaching an incomplete picture of salvation, for that was all he knew at the time. So two disciples, Priscilla and Aquila, took him aside *privately*—exactly as they should have done—and taught him a fuller, more complete doctrine of the gospel. **Apollos** correctly humbled himself to their teaching, absorbed the knowledge, and continued in his ministry, accomplishing awesome things for the church.

Bold, committed, powerful in his gospel presentation ... this was a man on fire for Christ and used by God to establish the church. His popularity only grew from there, so much so that believers in Corinth experienced schisms, disagreeing about which disciple was better to align themselves with:

> For when one says, "I am of Paul," and another, "I am of **Apollos**," are you not mere men? What then is **Apollos**? And what is Paul? Servants through whom you believed, even as the Lord gave opportunity to each one. I planted, **Apollos** watered,

but God was causing the growth. So then neither the one who plants nor the one who waters is anything, but God who causes the growth. Now he who plants and he who waters are one; but each will receive his own reward according to his own labor. For we are God's fellow workers; you are God's field, God's building.[336]

The Corinthian churches were immature by siding with one church leader over another to the point of arguing about it, and Paul rightly calls them out. But from this, **Apollos'** status as an authority in the early church is confirmed yet again. He was a strong leader, obviously well-loved by the people, very active in ministry, and in a strong ministerial relationship with Paul as he writes to Titus.

While we don't know with certainty what **Zenas the lawyer and Apollos** were doing or where they were going, these two men were traveling through Crete **on their way**. Again, it was a popular trade stop in the ancient world. In all likelihood, **Zenas** and **Apollos** were the ones who delivered Paul's letter to Titus for him.[337] Since Titus was settled in and knew Crete and its culture, and because he was their brother in Christ, he was to **diligently help** these two men, making sure **nothing is lacking for them.**

Diligently helping them seems to evoke a sense of urgency. Paul wanted their needs to be met quickly, so **Zenas** and **Apollos** could continue their journey without delay. In a time when communication and travel weren't nearly as immediate as they are today, any and all time they could save made a big difference. Seen in conjunction with the following verse about their people also learning **to engage in good deeds to meet pressing needs so that they will not be unfruitful,** Paul seems to be suggesting that "Titus will accomplish this by mobilizing the church to help … that house churches would fulfill their responsibility of extending hospitality to traveling Christians."[338]

The house churches of Crete were to do whatever they could to help in whatever ways **Zenas** and **Apollos** needed it. By doing so, they weren't just helping family members in the faith; they were also serving to advance the gospel and receiving an opportunity to live it out. There's little doubt those two men were on a specific assignment commissioned by Paul. Meeting their needs, the church would aid in their mission, thereby aiding the mission of the gospel.

Thus, Cretan Christians were to be prepared and ready to meet each other's needs as well as those of traveling missionaries and people who did not yet know Christ. This reflects one of the character traits of elders mentioned in the first list within this letter, for elders were to be **hospitable.** Hospitality involved, to an extent, living with an open-door policy, welcoming people and caring for them while they were under the roofs of believers.

Hospitality was just one way the people were to **learn to engage in good deeds and meet pressing needs.** Cretan believers most likely provided **Zenas and Apollos** with any supplies needed to carry them through the remainder of their journey—food, equipment, etc. But this directive of Paul isn't limited to those two traveling missionaries. Cretan believers were to put their faith to practice by **engaging in good deeds** always.

Cretan believers were **to learn** how to do good deeds by *doing* good deeds. There's hardly a better way to learn something than by doing it firsthand. We learn to swim by jumping in a pool and swimming; we learn to cook by cooking; we learn to write by writing; we learn to ski by skiing. The same can be said of our faith. We learn to live it by doing it—consistently, frequently, and eagerly.

Engage is the same word used in verse 8 of this chapter, when Paul told Titus to speak confidently of the truths he communicated so "those who have believed God will be careful to engage in good deeds." This repetition is not accidental. Paul knows he'd just written a general instruction for engaging in good deeds, and he now provides them with reinforcement and an opportunity to comply with **Zenas** and **Apollos.**

Believers adorn the Word of God by living it out personally and well as communally. Paul wrote frequently of an individual's need to achieve gospel-inspired character traits in his own life, trusting Titus to confirm it in his teachings. But the opportunity he gives the Cretan church to care for **Zenas** and **Apollos** reveals another stunning aspect to the practical application of faith—love and care for one another.

Putting faith into practice will inevitably impact those around us, for we don't grow in our character in a vacuum. Our character and faith grow as we live them out in the context of relationships. Let's consider Paul's directive for young women to be **kind** from chapter 2 verse 5 as an example. Kindness embodies a spirit of pleasantness that begins in our mind (making a decision to be kind instead of bitter or some other negative emotion), and filters out to our attitude, which immediately impacts those around us. We cannot exhibit kindness apart from relationships, for only when we're in contact with others can we have the opportunity to show kindness. The same can be said of nearly all character traits—love, being reverent, temperate, encouraging, pure, etc. We grow in these by living them out in our interactions with people around us.

That's one reason **good deeds** so often correspond with meeting **pressing needs.** The needs around us are often determined by our relationships— either intimate or cursory. A child needs extra attention during a season of heightened insecurity because of bullying at school. Our spouse needs more encouragement from us than usual because of the added stress he is experiencing at work. We commit to making meals once a week for friend from church who is struggling to make ends meet. We pray with a store clerk who is near tears when helping us check out. Needs are all around us, as our needs were all around Christ. Christ noticed and gave everything

He had to meet every one of our needs (giving us extra benefits of grace beyond that), even though we didn't ask for it. If He did that and we are in Him, it's our duty and joy to do the same for others. Needs surround us, and it's a privilege to look for them and meet them at every opportunity. By doing this, we **engage in good deeds** so we **will not be unfruitful.**

Producing fruit is a major theme throughout the New Testament, as it is in our Christian lives. If we are in Christ and are growing in our faith, we produce fruit (or evidence) of it. Christ gives us a beautiful illustration of the process of faith bearing fruit:

> "I am the true vine, and My Father is the vinedresser. Every branch in me that does not bear fruit, he takes away, and every branch that bears fruit, He prunes it so that it may bear more fruit. You are already clean because of the word which I have spoken to you. Abide in Me, and I in you. As the branch cannot bear fruit of itself unless it abides in the vine, so neither can you unless you abide in Me. I am the vine, you are the branches; he who abides in Me and I in him, he bears much fruit, for apart from Me you can do nothing … My Father is glorified by this, that you bear much fruit, and so prove to be My disciples.[339]

Fruit of eternal significance comes only when we abide and reside in Christ, who, with the Holy Spirit, keeps us abiding and residing in God the Father. Some examples of the kind of fruit produced in our lives:

> But the fruit of the Spirit is love, joy, peace, patience, kindness, goodness, faithfulness, gentleness, self-control …[340]

Again, these fruits are lived out in the context of relationships. They not only help us see the needs of others, but they also empower us to meet them, therefore making our faith fruitful and the gospel beautiful in our lives.

ALL WHO ARE WITH ME GREET YOU. GREET THOSE WHO LOVE US IN THE FAITH. GRACE BE WITH YOU ALL.

Speaking of relationships, Paul bolsters his final greeting to Titus by including **all who are with** him. We don't know how many that is (Titus probably didn't know the exact number either, due to the shifting nature of ministry positions and assignments). But Paul wanted Titus to know that the full force of gospel ministers with him were rooting for, supporting, encouraging, and thinking of Titus as they **greet** him through Paul's letter.

Likewise, Titus was to **greet those who love** Paul and all the other gospel ministers **in the faith.** The importance of community cannot be underestimated or over-communicated. While Titus did experience community with the Cretan believers, the depth probably wasn't the same as the community he experienced with Paul and other workers who'd dedicated their entire lives to the advancement of the gospel. He needed to stay connected to them, and reading even greetings from them would've strengthened and rejuvenated his spirit.

Community brings joy, as do their words of truth spoken in love. Paul ends his letter with **grace be with you all.** This is a common phrase with Paul, but its frequent use doesn't diminish the message it communicates: "a genuine prayer or blessing that desires for the recipients the full experience of God's gracious and loving presence (with all this entails)."[341] By extending the blessing to the Cretan believers by the inclusion of the word **all,** Paul vigorously reveals his love not just for Titus, but for all those in Christ on the island of Crete.

Because of the "moral, social, and ecclesiastical challenges facing the young Cretan churches, and given the goal of actualizing faith in dynamic Christian living that Paul has set before them, this wish for a holistic experience of God's grace was nothing less than a final prayer for strength in battle."[342] Titus was given a weighty assignment to establish the church on Crete. Paul knew the challenges, trusted and empowered Titus to rise up, and dedicated himself to the continued ministry of Titus as he carried out his mission. Most of all, Paul trusted Titus and the Cretan believers to God, knowing the relationship they experienced with Him first through Christ had satisfied and inspired them to experience it more deeply with one another. This intimate sense of community energized their faith, which caused it to be fruitful and emboldened them to make His Word beautiful to the world around them.

GROUP STUDY

INTRODUCTION

Faith comes to life in the context of community.

We are designed to live in relationships. Family, friends, coworkers, church family, hobby companions … regardless of framework, we thrive when we connect with others. No one enjoys being alone to the extent of feeling lonely. No one craves solitude when a thriving, God-motivated relationship has been experienced. Unfortunately, some relationships aren't what they should be. They leave us feeling discouraged, belittled, hurt, used, and disappointed. But when experienced as God intended them, relationships fuel, inspire, encourage, uplift, comfort, give a deep sense of belonging, and create avenues to exercise our faith.

- Tell us about a relationship in your past that wasn't so great, or a time in your life when you felt void of meaningful relationships.

- Share with us a relationship you've been in or are in now that's wonderful, and how it's impacted your life.

THE WORD

Paul's last comments to Titus reflect the understanding that humanity needs and thrives in community. When community is fractured, especially within the church, results can be devastating. But when relationships flourish, both with God and others, spirits are bolstered and inspired to carry on the work of the gospel with utmost joy.

> But avoid foolish controversies and genealogies and strife and disputes about the Law, for they are unprofitable and worthless. (Titus 3:9)

Reject a factious man after a first and second warning, knowing that such a man is perverted and is sinning, being self-condemned. (Titus 3:10-11)

When I send Artemas or Tychicus to you, make every effort to come to me at Nicopolis, for I have decided to spend the winter there. Diligently help Zenas the lawyer and Apollos on their way so that nothing is lacking for them. Our people must also learn to engage in good deeds to meet pressing needs, so that they will not be unfruitful. All who are with me greet you. Greet those who love us in the faith. Grace be with you all. (Titus 3:12-15)

- What four things was Titus to avoid (and instruct Cretan believers to avoid by extension)?

    - _____

    - _____

    - _____

    - _____

- Read Titus 3:10-11 and Matthew 18:15-17. What was the process of confrontation supposed to look like?

    - Why do you think that method is important?

- Why would Paul send either Artemas or Tychicus to Crete?

    - Who would benefit from that, and how?

- How was helping Zenas and Apollos an opportunity to "engage in good deeds"?

    - What's the relationship between good deeds and being in community?

APPLY

For we are His workmanship, created in Christ Jesus for good works,
which God prepared beforehand so that we would walk in them.
The Apostle Paul, Ephesians 2:10

Let us hold fast the confession of our hope without wavering, for He who
promised is faithful; and let us consider how to stimulate one another to
love and good deeds.
The Author of Hebrews, Hebrews 10:23-24

Our faith is stagnant unless we practice it in our daily lives. The majority of
such practice occurs within the context of our relationships. For example, we
grow in love by first understanding it (as God loves us), then by applying it
(by loving other people). We grow in kindness by learning of God's kindness,
then with that as our motivation, extending kindness to others. The same can
be said of any virtue or character trait. As we grow in our faith, we see needs
around us and meet them by putting our beliefs into practice.

- What are the different relational communities in your life right now?

  - Which ones actively draw you closer to God?

  - Do any relationships distract or even prevent you from
    growing closer to God?

    - What are some practical, God-honoring ways to go about
      redirecting, temporarily suspending, or even severing that
      relationship?

  - In what ways can you begin prioritizing God in other
    relationships, if only from your vantage point?

- In what ways can you put your faith into action to better meet
  the needs of those around you?

Conclusion

What a letter! Paul wrote his letter to Titus knowing Titus was not the only one who would benefit from the truths presented. But not even Paul could possibly imagine how God would use it in the lives of multitudes spanning countless generations.

He began with a lengthy introduction, reminding Titus and any other future reader of his identity as **a bond-servant of God and an apostle of Jesus Christ.** The mission of his apostleship was to further the faith, knowledge of truth, and godliness in believers. This was founded upon **the hope of eternal life** promised and guaranteed by God Himself, **who cannot lie.** Paul writes to Titus, a man whom he loved as his own child and invested in mightily through years of ministry together.

Titus served the Lord faithfully, and Paul trusted him implicitly to carry on the gospel work in his absence. Titus did so on the island of Crete by setting **in order what remains and appoint[ing] elders in every city.** Considering the size and grotesque moral depravity of Crete, this was no easy task. But Paul knew Titus could do it, empowered by the Holy Spirit and encouraged by his mentor, which he did plentifully.

Establishing elders was a weighty task, for candidates needed to be men **above reproach** in every area of their lives, including their families, individual character, and commitment to ministry within the church. These men were faithful leaders and especially needed because there were **many rebellious men** present within the church, and they actively led believers astray **for the sake of sordid gain.** Titus was to identify both kinds of leaders in the church, investing into elders and reproving rebellious leaders **severely so that they may be sound in the faith** eventually.

Standing in stark contrast to leaders who were **detestable and disobedient and worthless for any good deed,** Titus was to **speak the things which are fitting for sound doctrine.** This included, but was certainly not limited to, lists of character traits to be present within individual groupings of people—older men, older women, young women, young men, and bondslaves. Each of these groupings received specific instructions from Paul, to be taught and reinforced by Titus, who was to lead by example. Living out their faith was key to adorning the Word of God with their lives—making it beautiful, attractive, and desirable to those around them.

Obedience to all these directives was to be motivated by the gospel, **for the grace of God has appeared bringing salvation to all men.** This grace inspired and instructed believers to actively deny their former, worldly desires in order to pursue righteousness and godly living as they await the second coming of Jesus Christ. Jesus gave up everything in order to save us, make us His, and enable us to be **zealous for good deeds.** Good deeds bearing any eternal weight are but grateful responses for what Christ has done, is doing, and will do when He returns.

Cretan believers (like us) needed to be reminded of these truths frequently, especially considering the hideousness of their surrounding culture. Part of Titus' ministry was reminding them all to honor God in their perspectives and subsequent behaviors toward authorities and others in public, **showing consideration for all men.**

Such consideration stemmed from being reminded of their own pasts, how we as believers **also once were foolish ourselves,** rotting in our own putrid decay of sin that put God forever out of our reach (and desire). **But** (and oh, how we love when God uses "buts" in Scripture!) God intervened and **saved us, not on the basis of deeds which we have done in righteousness, but according to His mercy ...** through the work of the Holy Spirit and **according to the hope of eternal life,** security for all those who believe.

By reminding the Cretan believers of their sordid pasts and God's divine, love-inspired intervention on their behalves, Titus was fulfilling his duty in advancing the gospel of Jesus Christ. Paul reminded him to prioritize community among believers, first by avoiding **foolish controversies** and other distracting nonsense, then by purging any **factious man** found among them.

Paul concludes his letter by pleading for Titus to come to him, which would provide Titus with the rest and rejuvenation that comes from experiencing deep community among gospel-consumed peers. He also provided an opportunity for Titus and the Cretan Christians to **engage in good deeds** by meeting the **pressing needs** of traveling missionaries. They would all work together in community to help the missionaries, thereby aiding the expansion of the gospel and living out their faith in a way that adorned the doctrine they had come to believe.

This powerful letter contains profound theology and practical help for every Christian in their pursuit of embracing the gospel. When our actions are fueled by sound doctrine and conducted properly within the context of relationships, God is honored, His Word is made beautiful, and others are drawn to Him, which glorifies Him all the more.

Bibliography

Barclay, William. *The Letters to Timothy, Titus, and Philemon.* Louisville, Kentucky: Westminster John Knox Press, 1957.

Blaesing, C. "Dispensation, Dispensationalism," in *Evangelical Dictionary of Theology Second Edition,* ed. Walter A. Elwell. Grand Rapids, Michigan: Baker Book House Company, 1984.

Calder, W. M. "Crete." *Bible Atlas.* Accessed 3 Feb. 2018, bibleatlas.org/crete.htm.

Dibelius, Martin, and Conzelmann, Hans. *The Pastoral Epistles.* Minneapolis, MN: Fortress Press, 1989.

Douglas, J. D. and Merrill C. Tenney. *New International Bible Dictionary.* Grand Rapids, Michigan: Zondervan, 1987.

Fairbarn, P. *Commentary on the Pastoral Epistles.* Grand Rapids, Michigan: Zondervan, 1956.

Fee, Gordon D. *1 & 2 Timothy, Titus.* Grand Rapids, Michigan: Baker Books, 1984.

Gray, Patrick. "The Liar Paradox and the Letter to Titus," *CBQ* 69, 2007.

Hiebert, D. Edmond. *Titus.* Grand Rapids, Michigan: Zondervan, 1978.

Hughes, R. Kent, and Chapell, Bryan. *1-2 Timothy and Titus: To Guard the Deposit.* Wheaton, Illinois: Crossway, 2012.

Jeffers, James S. *The Greco-Roman World of the New Testament Era: Exploring the Background of Early Christianity.* Downers Grove, Illinois: InterVarsity Press, 1999.

Keller, Timothy. *The Prodigal God.* New York, New York: Dutton, 2008.

Kostenberger, Andreas J. *Commentary on 1-2 Timothy & Titus.* Nashville, Tennessee: B&H Publishing Group, 2017.

Lea, Thomas D., and Hayne P. Griffin. *1, 2 Timothy, Titus.* Vol. 34, Nashville, Tennessee: B&H Publishing Group, 1992.

Liefeld, Walter L. *The NIV Application Commentary: 1 & 2 Timothy, Titus.* Grand Rapids, Michigan: Zondervan, 1999.

Lloyd-Jones, D. Martyn. *Studies in the Sermon on the Mount.* Grand Rapids, Michigan: Wm. B. Eerdmans Publishing Company, 1976.

Stott, John R. W. *The Message of 1 Timothy & Titus.* Downers Grove, Illinois: InterVarsity Press, 1996.

Towner, Philip H. *1-2 Timothy & Titus.* Downers Grove, Illinois: InterVarsity Press, 1994.

Towner, Philip H. *The Letters to Timothy and Titus.* Grand Rapids, MI: Wm. B. Eerdmans Publishing Co, 2006.

Young, Robert. *Young's Analytical Concordance to the Bible.* Peabody, Massachusetts: Hendrickson Publishers, 1984.

Endnotes

CHAPTER ONE

[1] Towner, Philip H., *The Letters to Timothy and Titus* (Grand Rapids, MI: Wm. B. Eerdmans Publishing Co, 2006), 9. The first people to doubt the authenticity of Paul's authorship were F. D. E. Schleiermacher, J. G. Eichhorn, and F. C. Baur. However, these men weren't around (and thus didn't question it) until the nineteenth century.

[2] Acts 6:8-8:3.

[3] Acts 9:2.

[4] Acts 8:3.

[5] Galatians 1:13-14.

[6] Acts 9.

[7] Galatians 1:13-2:1.

[8] Acuna, Kristen. "The 33 Most Expensive Movie Props Ever Sold." *Business Insider.* August 18, 2014. Accessed January 30, 2018. http://www.businessinsider.com/most-expensive-movie-props-ever-2014-8.

[9] Towner, *The Letters to Timothy and Titus*, 665. Word doesn't allow us to use the "comments" feature in endnotes. (I don't know why.) Therefore, I'll put my comments within the text, like this. Chicago Manual of Style says this is the format for shortened citations for books.

[10] Jeffers, James S., *The Greco-Roman World of the New Testament Era: Exploring the Background of Early Christianity* (Downers Grove, Illinois: InterVarsity Press, 1999), 223.

[11] Jeffers, *The Greco-Roman World*, 223-224.

[12] Leviticus 25:46.

[13] Jeffers, *The Greco-Roman World*, 226.

[14] Jeffers, *The Greco-Roman World*, 222.

[15] Deuteronomy 15:17.

[16] Towner, Philip H., *1-2 Timothy & Titus* (Downers Grove, Illinois: InterVarsity Press, 1994), 218.

[17] Acts 9:15.

[18] Fee, Gordon D., *1 & 2 Timothy, Titus* (Grand Rapids, Michigan: Baker Books, 1984), 168.

[19] Hebrews 11:1, 3.

[20] Romans 8:28.

[21] Ephesians 1:3-14.

[22] Lea, Thomas D., and Hayne P. Griffin, *1, 2 Timothy, Titus* Vol. 34 (Nashville, Tennessee: B&H Publishing Group, 1992), 266.

[23] Kostenberger, Andreas J., *Commentary on 1-2 Timothy & Titus* (Nashville, Tennessee: B&H Publishing Group, 2017), 308.

[24] Stott, John R. W., *The Message of 1 Timothy & Titus,* (Downers Grove, Illinois: InterVarsity Press, 1996) 169.

[25] Hebrews 6:17-19a.

[26] Towner, *The Letters to Timothy and Titus,* 670.

[27] Genesis 3:16.

[28] Kostenberger, *Commentary on 1-2 Timothy & Titus,* 309.

[29] Towner, *The Letters to Timothy and Titus,* 674.

[30] Titles found in the following verses, respectively: 2 Corinthians 2:13, 8:23; Titus 1:4.

[31] Acts 13:51.

[32] God chose Israel to be His mouthpiece to the world, beginning with Abraham in Genesis 12 and echoed throughout the remainder of the Old Testament (Psalm 78 is a good example as well).

[33] Read Acts 10 for a better understanding of how this unfolded. The whole book of Acts would be ideal too.

[34] Romans 10:13.

[35] The other two pastoral letters are 1 & 2 Timothy.

[36] Romans 1:7, 1 Corinthians 1:3, 2 Corinthians 1:2, Galatians 1:3, Ephesians 1:2, Philippians 1:2, 2 Thessalonians 1:2, Philemon 1:3.

[37] Douglas, J. D. and Merrill C. Tenney, *New International Bible Dictionary* (Grand Rapids, Michigan: Zondervan, 1987), 401.

[38] Philippians 4:7.

39 Hughes, R. Kent, and Chapell, Bryan. *1-2 Timothy and Titus: To Guard the Deposit.* (Wheaton, Illinois: Crossway, 2012) 304.

40 1 Corinthians 11:1.

CHAPTER TWO

41 Calder, W. M., "Crete." *Bible Atlas.* Accessed 3 Feb. 2018, bibleatlas.org/crete.htm.

42 Towner, *The Letters to Timothy and Titus*, 678.

43 Douglas and Tenney, *New International Bible Dictionary*, 241.

44 Towner, *The Letters to Timothy and Titus*, 678.

45 John 21:24-25.

46 Acts 14:23; Towner, *The Letters to Timothy and Titus*, 679.

47 This is not the only list of elder/overseer qualifications in Scripture. See 1 Timothy 3:1-7 for another, very similar list.

48 Stott, *The Message of 1 Timothy & Titus*, 174.

49 Stott, *The Message of 1 Timothy & Titus*, 174.

50 Young, Robert, *Young's Analytical Concordance to the Bible* (Peabody, Massachusetts: Hendrickson Publishers, 1984), 97.

51 Lea and Griffin, *1, 2 Timothy, Titus*, 279.

52 Barclay, William, *The Letters to Timothy, Titus, and Philemon* (Louisville, Kentucky: Westminster John Knox Press, 1957), 265.

53 Towner, *The Letters to Timothy and Titus*, 682.

[54] Young, *Young's Analytical Concordance to the Bible*, 86, 87, 324, 325.

[55] Towner, *The Letters to Timothy and Titus*, 683-684.

[56] Stott, *The Message of 1 Timothy & Titus*, 176.

[57] Stott, *The Message of 1 Timothy & Titus*, 176.

[58] Read John chapter 1, 3:19-21, 5:35, 8:12, 9:5, 11:9-10, 12:35-46 for more references showing how Jesus (and we in Him) are light in the world.

[59] Job 1:21.

[60] Towner, *The Letters to Timothy and Titus*, 687.

[61] Ephesians 4:26-27.

[62] Lea and Griffin, *1, 2 Timothy, Titus*, 284.

[63] Fee, *1 & 2 Timothy, Titus*, 81.

[64] For more information, do a simple word search for "house" in the New Testament, particularly in Acts. Individual homes played a crucial role in the development of the early church. Its existence depended largely on the hospitality of the hosts.

[65] Towner, *The Letters to Timothy and Titus*, 689.

[66] Lea and Griffin, *1, 2 Timothy, Titus*, 284.

[67] Towner, *1-2 Timothy & Titus*, 228.

[68] Now that we have the completed canon of Scripture, the Holy Spirit does not reveal new revelation (new to us at certain times in our lives, perhaps, but nothing new that isn't already contained within the pages of God's Word).

[69] Barclay, *The Letters to Timothy, Titus, and Philemon*, 273.

[70] Lea and Griffin, *1, 2 Timothy, Titus*, 289.

[71] Towner, *The Letters to Timothy and Titus*, 700.

[72] Deuteronomy 18:20.

[73] Kostenberger, *Commentary on 1-2 Timothy & Titus*, 320.

[74] Gray, Patrick, "The Liar Paradox and the Letter to Titus," *The Catholic Biblical Quarterly* 69 No. 2 (2007): 303.

[75] Kostenberger, *Commentary on 1-2 Timothy & Titus*, 320.

[76] Barclay, *The Letters to Timothy, Titus, and Philemon*, 274.

[77] Barclay, *The Letters to Timothy, Titus, and Philemon*, 274.

[78] Read Matthew 23 for a more in-depth look at Jesus' issues with the Pharisees' self-righteousness.

[79] Read Leviticus 11 for a more thorough list of foods that God deemed clean and unclean.

[80] Matthew 15:11.

[81] Fee, *1 & 2 Timothy, Titus*, 182.

[82] The creation account in Genesis 1 and 2 is a fascinating read for an example of this. "God caused to grow every tree that is pleasing to the sight and good for food ..." (2:9) Beauty isn't necessary, but it does reflect God and is a gift we can and do enjoy.

CHAPTER THREE

[83] Towner, *The Letters to Timothy and Titus*, 720.

[84] Lea and Griffin, *1, 2 Timothy, Titus*, 297.

[85] Hughes and Chapell, *1-2 Timothy and Titus*, 359.

[86] Fee, *1 & 2 Timothy, Titus*, 81.

[87] Barclay, *The Letters to Timothy, Titus, and Philemon*.

[88] Philippians 4:8.

[89] Barclay, *The Letters to Timothy, Titus, and Philemon*, 278.

[90] Towner, *The Letters to Timothy and Titus*, 720.

[91] Stott, *The Message of 1 Timothy & Titus*, 187.

[92] Hebrews 11:1.

[93] Towner, *The Letters to Timothy and Titus*, 721.

[94] Hebrews 11:6.

[95] 1 John 4:8.

[96] 1 John 4:7-12.

[97] NLT and NET Bible translations, respectively.

[98] Fee, *1 & 2 Timothy, Titus*, 186.

[99] Fee, *1 & 2 Timothy, Titus*, 186.

[100] Hebrews 7:22b-28.

[101] 1 Peter 2:5, 9.

[102] Proverbs 20:19.

[103] Lea and Griffin, *1, 2 Timothy, Titus*. 299.

[104] Galatians 5:16.

[105] 1 Timothy 2:9-15. I highly suggest reading that with the help of numerous conservative evangelical commentaries.

[106] One fabulous resource is *Recovering Biblical Manhood and Womanhood: A Response to Evangelical Feminism* edited by John Piper and Wayne Grudem, 1991.

[107] Ephesians 5:22-24.

[108] Ephesians 5:25-33.

[109] Lea and Griffin, *1, 2 Timothy, Titus*, 300.

[110] Towner, *The Letters to Timothy and Titus*, 726.

[111] Towner, *1-2 Timothy & Titus*, 238.

[112] I Corinthians 13:4-8a.

[113] Proverbs 12:4 and 31:10.

[114] Hughes and Chapell, *1-2 Timothy and Titus*, 362.

[115] Towner, *The Letters to Timothy and Titus*, 727.

[116] 2 Corinthians 10:5.

[117] Hughes and Chapell, *1-2 Timothy and Titus*, 362.

[118] Hosea 4:12.

[119] Psalm 115:4-8.

[120] Dibelius, Martin, and Conzelmann, Hans, *The Pastoral Epistles* (Minneapolis, MN: Fortress Press, 1989), 141.

[121] Lea and Griffin, *1, 2 Timothy, Titus*, 301.

[122] Jeffers, *The Greco-Roman World*, 249.

[123] Lydia's story in Acts 16 is an excellent example.

[124] 1 Corinthians 7:13-14.

[125] Elders in 1:8, older men in 2:2, and young women in 2:5.

[126] Stott, *The Message of 1 Timothy & Titus*, 189.

[127] This supports our theory that previous instruction to young men was brief because Titus was one of them.

[128] Kostenberger, *Commentary on 1-2 Timothy & Titus*, 335.

[129] ESV Bible translation.

[130] Towner, *The Letters to Timothy and Titus*, 731.

[131] Fee, *1 & 2 Timothy, Titus*, 189.

[132] Barclay, *The Letters to Timothy, Titus, and Philemon*, 284.

[133] Stott, *The Message of 1 Timothy & Titus*, 190.

[134] Towner, *The Letters to Timothy and Titus*, 732.

[135] Lea and Griffin, *1, 2 Timothy, Titus*, 304.

[136] Lea and Griffin, *1, 2 Timothy, Titus*, 305.

[137] Towner, *The Letters to Timothy and Titus*, 734.

[138] Hughes and Chapell, *1-2 Timothy and Titus*, 365.

[139] Revelation 5:11-13.

[140] Revelation 5:9.

[141] Colossians 3:22-24.

[142] Lea and Griffin, *1, 2 Timothy, Titus*, 308.

[143] Liefeld, Walter L., *The NIV Application Commentary: 1 & 2 Timothy, Titus* (Grand Rapids, Michigan: Zondervan, 1999), 329.

[144] Fee, *1 & 2 Timothy, Titus,* 190.

[145] John 12:6.

[146] Matthew 6:24.

[147] Stott, *The Message of 1 Timothy & Titus*, 191.

[148] Lea and Griffin, *1, 2 Timothy, Titus*, 308.

CHAPTER FOUR

[149] Galatians 3:2-3.

[150] Psalm 90:4.

[151] Romans 4:17b.

[152] Ephesians 2:1-2, 4-5.

[153] Colossians 2:13.

[154] Shorter Westminster Catechism, the Chief End of Man.

[155] Romans 6:23.

[156] Ephesians 2:8-9.

[157] Romans 10:8-10.

[158] John 3:16-17.

[159] John 1:11-12.

[160] 1 Timothy 2:4.

[161] Young, *Young's Analytical Concordance to the Bible*, 963.

[162] Towner, *1-2 Timothy & Titus*, 244.

[163] Reference Acts 17:21 and Paul's subsequent sermon to Athenians.

[164] Towner, *The Letters to Timothy and Titus*, 747.

[165] Towner, *The Letters to Timothy and Titus*, 748.

[166] Romans 8:5-8.

[167] Liefeld, *The NIV Application Commentary: 1 & 2 Timothy, Titus*, 339.

[168] Ephesians 4:21-24 (emphasis added).

[169] Barclay, *The Letters to Timothy, Titus, and Philemon*, 288.

[170] Douglas and Tenney, *New International Bible Dictionary*, 863.

[171] Romans 5:17-21.

[172] Fee, *1 & 2 Timothy, Titus*, 195.

[173] John 12:46.

[174] John 8:12.

[175] John 3:21.

[176] Matthew 5:16.

[177] Blaesing, C., "Dispensation, Dispensationalism" *Evangelical Dictionary of Theology Second Edition* ed. Walter A. Elwell (Grand Rapids, Michigan: Baker Book House Company, 1984), 343-344.

[178] 1 Corinthians 13:12.

[179] Romans 8:34.

[180] John 14:26.

[181] John 16:7.

[182] Young, Robert, "Index-Lexicon to the New Testament," *Young's Analytical Concordance to the Bible* (Peabody, Massachusetts: Hendrickson Publishers, 1984), 87.

[183] Philippians 3:20-21.

[184] Hebrews 9:28.

[185] 1 Corinthians 4:5.

[186] Mark 13:32.

[187] Matthew 25:13.

[188] Matthew 5:3-12a.

[189] Lloyd-Jones, D. Martyn, *Studies in the Sermon on the Mount* (Grand Rapids, Michigan: Wm. B. Eerdmans Publishing Company, 1976), 24.

[190] Acts 1:11.

[191] Harrison, E. F. "Glory," *Evangelical Dictionary of Theology Second Edition* ed. Walter A. Elwell (Grand Rapids, Michigan: Baker Book House Company, 1984) 484.

[192] Douglas and Tenney, *New International Bible Dictionary*, 392.

[193] Ex 33:18-23; 34:29.

[194] Isaiah 6:1-4.

[195] Hebrews 1:3.

[196] John 1:14.

[197] Stott, *The Message of 1 Timothy & Titus*, 194.

[198] Hebrews 4:15.

[199] Colossians 2:13-14.

[200] Philippians 2:6-8.

[201] Romans 5:12.

[202] Matthew 5:17.

[203] Romans 8:3-4.

[204] Exodus 19:5-6.

[205] Micah 7:18.

[206] Malachi 3:17.

[207] 1 Peter 2:9.

[208] Hebrews 13:5.

[209] Romans 8:35-39.

[210] Matthew 13:44-46.

[211] Towner, *The Letters to Timothy and Titus*, 766.

[212] Towner, *The Letters to Timothy and Titus*, 767.

CHAPTER FIVE

[213] Judges 3:7.

[214] Psalm 78:11.

[215] Psalm 106:13.

[216] Judges 8:34.

[217] Deuteronomy 32:7.

[218] 1 Chronicles 16:12.

[219] 1 Chronicles 16:15.

[220] Isaiah 46:9.

[221] Lea and Griffin, *1, 2 Timothy, Titus*, 317.

[222] Quote attributed to Polybius, restated in Barclay, William, *The Letters to Timothy, Titus, and Philemon*, 290.

[223] Romans 13:1.

[224] Colossians 1:16.

[225] Hughes and Chapell, *1-2 Timothy and Titus*, 390.

[226] Matthew 22:15-22.

[227] Acts 12:2.

[228] 2 Corinthians 10:5.

[229] Lea and Griffin, *1, 2 Timothy, Titus*, 318.

[230] Matthew 5:41.

[231] Lloyd-Jones, *Studies in the Sermon on the Mount*, 252.

[232] Young, *Young's Analytical Concordance to the Bible*, 923.

[233] Towner, *The Letters to Timothy and Titus*, 772.

[234] James 3:3-5.

[235] Ephesians 4:15-16; 25.

[236] Liefeld, *The NIV Application Commentary: 1 & 2 Timothy, Titus*, 349.

[237] James 4:1-2a, 4.

[238] St. Augustine of Hippo's Confessions, Lib 1,1-2,2.5,5: CSEL 33, 1-5.

[239] Towner, *The Letters to Timothy and Titus*, 773.

[240] Lea and Griffin, *1, 2 Timothy, Titus*, 319.

[241] Barclay, *The Letters to Timothy, Titus, and Philemon*, 291.

[242] Lea and Griffin, *1, 2 Timothy, Titus*, 319.

[243] Vine's Expository Dictionary of New Testament Words, accessed February 16, 2018, www.blueletterbible.org.

[244] Matthew 11:28-29.

[245] Matthew 21:5.

[246] 2 Corinthians 10:1.

[247] Galatians 5:22-23.

[248] Galatians 6:1.

[249] Ephesians 4:2.

[250] Colossians 3:12.

[251] 1 Timothy 6:11.

[252] Young, *Young's Analytical Concordance to the Bible*, 361.

[253] Stott, *The Message of 1 Timothy & Titus*, 202.

[254] Towner, *The Letters to Timothy and Titus*, 775.

[255] 1 Corinthians 1:18-21, 26-27.

[256] Kostenberger, *Commentary on 1-2 Timothy & Titus*, 346.

[257] Titus 1:16.

[258] Jeremiah 17:9-10.

[259] Romans 1:18-20.

[260] Genesis 3:1-7a.

[261] Matthew 4:1-11.

[262] Towner, *The Letters to Timothy and Titus*, 777.

[263] Stott, *The Message of 1 Timothy & Titus*, 202.

[264] John 15:13, 1 John 3:16a.

[265] John 13:35.

[266] Lea and Griffin, *1, 2 Timothy, Titus*, 320.

[267] Towner, *1-2 Timothy & Titus*, 244.

[268] Lea and Griffin, *1, 2 Timothy, Titus*, 321.

[269] Lea and Griffin, *1, 2 Timothy, Titus*, 321.

[270] Romans 2:4.

[271] Ephesians 2:7.

[272] Colossians 3:12.

[273] Towner, *The Letters to Timothy and Titus*, 778.

[274] Towner, *The Letters to Timothy and Titus*, 778.

[275] 1 Corinthians 9:19-23a.

[276] Isaiah 64:6.

[277] Matthew 6:1-4.

[278] Luke 15:11-32.

[279] Keller, Timothy, *The Prodigal God.* (New York, New York: Dutton, 2008), 38, 39.

[280] Read Leviticus 13 for lots of examples.

[281] Romans 6:3-11.

[282] Fee, *1 & 2 Timothy, Titus*, 205.

[283] Stott, *The Message of 1 Timothy & Titus*, 205.

[284] John 3:3-7.

[285] Romans 12:2.

[286] Ephesians 1:13-14.

[287] Packer, J. I. "Justification" *Evangelical Dictionary of Theology Second Edition* ed. Walter A. Elwell (Grand Rapids, Michigan: Baker Academic, 1984), 643.

[288] John 1:16.

[289] Keller, *The Prodigal God*, 84.

[290] Romans 8:16-17a.

[291] Lea and Griffin, *1, 2 Timothy, Titus*, 325.

[292] 2 Timothy 3:16.

CHAPTER SIX

[293] Fee, *1 & 2 Timothy, Titus*, 211.

[294] 2 Timothy 2:23.

[295] 1 Timothy 6:3-5.

[296] 1 Timothy 1:3b-4.

[297] 2 Timothy 2:16.

[298] 2 Timothy 2:14.

[299] Towner, *The Letters to Timothy and Titus*, 795.

[300] Towner, *The Letters to Timothy and Titus*, 795.

[301] Remember, the book of Revelation is a vision given to an individual (the apostle John), who described things he'd never seen before. Therefore, he had no vocabulary to describe it accurately. How would someone in ancient times describe a helicopter or a computer? That's what John faced.

He was describing a vision full of objects he had no frame of reference for, which is one reason why understanding and interpreting the details of Revelation is so difficult.

[302] Matthew 1:1-17.

[303] Towner, *The Letters to Timothy and Titus*, 795.

[304] Young, *Young's Analytical Concordance to the Bible*, 941.

[305] John 13:34-35.

[306] John 15:12.

[307] Towner, *The Letters to Timothy and Titus*, 796.

[308] Fairbarn, P., *Commentary on the Pastoral Epistles* (Grand Rapids, Michigan: Zondervan, 1956), 301.

[309] Stott, *The Message of 1 Timothy & Titus*, 210.

[310] Fee, *1 & 2 Timothy, Titus*, 211.

[311] John 17:19-23.

[312] Towner, *The Letters to Timothy and Titus*, 797.

[313] Titus 1:13.

[314] Hiebert, D. Edmond, *Titus* (Grand Rapids, Michigan: Zondervan, 1978), 448.

[315] Towner, *The Letters to Timothy and Titus*, 797-8.

[316] Lea and Griffin. *1, 2 Timothy, Titus*, 328.

[317] Fee, *1 & 2 Timothy, Titus*, 212.

[318] Douglas and Tenney, *New International Bible Dictionary*, 946.

[319] Romans 3:23.

[320] Fee, *1 & 2 Timothy, Titus*, 212.

[321] Matthew 18:15-17.

[322] Kostenberger, *Commentary on 1-2 Timothy & Titus*, 353.

[323] Acts 20:4, emphasis mine.

[324] Ephesians 6:21, emphasis mine.

[325] Colossians 4:7, emphasis mine.

[326] 2 Timothy 4:12, emphasis mine.

[327] Towner, *The Letters to Timothy and Titus*, 800.

[328] Towner, *The Letters to Timothy and Titus*, 800.

[329] Kostenberger, *Commentary on 1-2 Timothy & Titus*, 353.

[330] Kostenberger, *Commentary on 1-2 Timothy & Titus*, 353.

[331] Kostenberger, *Commentary on 1-2 Timothy & Titus*, 353.

[332] Kostenberger, *Commentary on 1-2 Timothy & Titus*, 353.

[333] Lea and Griffin, *1, 2 Timothy, Titus*, 332.

[334] Acts 18:24-28, emphasis mine.

[335] Kostenberger, *Commentary on 1-2 Timothy & Titus*, 354.

[336] 1 Corinthians 3:4-9, emphasis mine.

[337] Kostenberger, *Commentary on 1-2 Timothy & Titus*, 354.

[338] Towner, *The Letters to Timothy and Titus*, 801.

[339] John 15:1-5, 8.

[340] Galatians 5:22-23a.

[341] Towner, *The Letters to Timothy and Titus*, 805.

[342] Towner, *The Letters to Timothy and Titus*, 805.

www.ingramcontent.com/pod-product-compliance
Lightning Source LLC
LaVergne TN
LVHW081327060426
835513LV00012B/1216